# KEY CASES
# EQUITY & TRUSTS

2nd edition

Judith Bray

HODDER EDUCATION
AN HACHETTE UK COMPANY

Orders: please contact Bookpoint Ltd, 130 Milton Park, Abingdon, Oxon OX14 4SB. Telephone: (44) 01235 827720. Fax: (44) 01235 400454. Lines are open from 9.00 – 5.00, Monday to Saturday, with a 24 hour message answering service. You can also order through our website www.hoddereducation.co.uk

If you have any comments to make about this, or any of our other titles, please send them to educationenquiries@hodder.co.uk

*British Library Cataloguing in Publication Data*
A catalogue record for this title is available from the British Library

ISBN 978 1 444 13782 8

First Edition published 2006
This Edition published 2011
Impression number 10 9 8 7 6 5 4 3 2 1
Year 2014 2013 2012 2011



Typeset by Transet Limited, Coventry, England.
Printed in Great Britain for Hodder Education, an Hachette UK Company, 338 Euston Road, London NW1 3BH by CPI Cox & Wyman Ltd, Reading, RG1 8EX.

# Contents

# Table of cases

# Preface

The Key Cases series is designed to give a clear understanding of important cases. This is useful when studying a new topic and invaluable as a revision aid.

Each case is broken down into fact and law. In addition, many cases are extended by the use of important extracts from the judgment or by comment or by highlighting problems. In some instances students are reminded that there is a link to other cases or material. If the link case is in another part of the same Key Cases book, the reference will be clearly shown. Some links will be to additional cases or materials that do not feature in the book.

To give a clear layout, symbols have been used at the start of each component of the case. The symbols are:

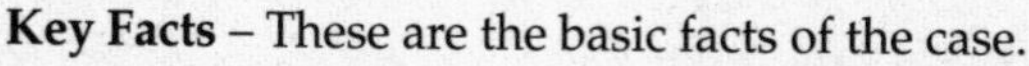

**Key Facts** – These are the basic facts of the case.

**Key Law** – This is the major principle of law in the case, the *ratio decidendi*.

**Key Judgment** – This is an actual extract from a judgment made on the case.

**Key Comment** – Influential or appropriate comments made on the case.

**Key Problem** – Apparent inconsistencies or difficulties in the law.

**Key Link** – This indicates other cases which should be considered with this case.

The Key Link symbol alerts readers to links within the book and also to cases and other material especially statutory provisions which is not included.

At the start of each chapter there are mind maps highlighting the main cases and points of law. In addition, within most chapters, one or two of the most important cases are boxed to identify them and stress their importance.

Each Key Case book can be used in conjunction with the Key Facts book on the same subject. Equally they can be used as additional material to support any other textbook.

The law is stated as I believe it to be on 31st January 2011.

Judith Bray

# 1

# The Definition of Equity

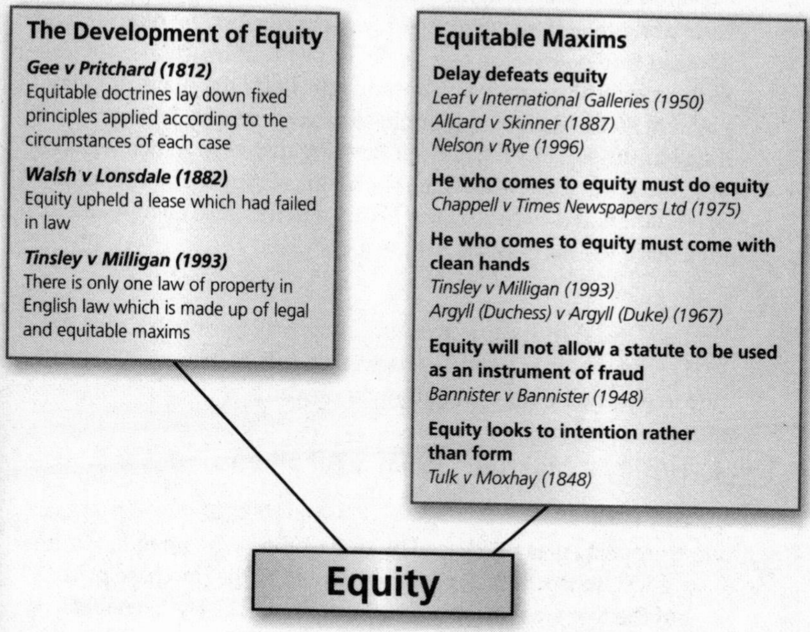

**The Development of Equity**

***Gee v Pritchard (1812)***
Equitable doctrines lay down fixed principles applied according to the circumstances of each case

***Walsh v Lonsdale (1882)***
Equity upheld a lease which had failed in law

***Tinsley v Milligan (1993)***
There is only one law of property in English law which is made up of legal and equitable maxims

**Equitable Maxims**

**Delay defeats equity**
*Leaf v International Galleries (1950)*
*Allcard v Skinner (1887)*
*Nelson v Rye (1996)*

**He who comes to equity must do equity**
*Chappell v Times Newspapers Ltd (1975)*

**He who comes to equity must come with clean hands**
*Tinsley v Milligan (1993)*
*Argyll (Duchess) v Argyll (Duke) (1967)*

**Equity will not allow a statute to be used as an instrument of fraud**
*Bannister v Bannister (1948)*

**Equity looks to intention rather than form**
*Tulk v Moxhay (1848)*

**Equity**

## 1.1 The development of equity

HC Gee v Pritchard (1818) 2 Swan 402

**Key Judgment**
**Lord Eldon:** '…The doctrines of the Court of Chancery ought to be well settled, and made as uniform, almost as those of the common law, laying down fixed principles, but taking care that they are to be applied according to the circumstances of each case…nothing would inflict on me greater pain in quitting this place than the recollection that I had done anything to justify the reproach that the equity of this court varies like the Chancellor's foot.'

## Walsh v Lonsdale (1882) 21 Ch D 9

**Key Facts**

The defendant agreed to grant the plaintiff a legal lease of a weaving mill with the rent payable in advance, but it was not executed so it was an agreement for a lease rather than a legal lease and took effect in equity only. Nevertheless the plaintiff was allowed into possession and began to pay rent in arrears, consistent with a periodic tenancy at common law. Later the plaintiff failed to pay rent so the defendant sought to recover rent by trying to claim the plaintiff's goods for himself (levying distress), which was only possible if the lease was legal. The Court of Appeal held that the defendant had a right to do so because in this case an agreement for a lease was as good as a lease itself.

**Key Law**

Under s 25(11) Judicature Act 1873 (now s 49 Supreme Court Act 1981) when there is a conflict between a rule at common law and a rule in equity the rule in equity will prevail.

## (HL) Tinsley v Milligan [1993] 3 All ER 65

**Key Facts**

A property was purchased by two women who intended to run a guest house. Both parties contributed to the purchase price but the title was registered in the name of Tinsley to enable Milligan to claim social security benefits dishonestly. When the relationship broke down Milligan claimed an equitable interest under a resulting trust. Tinsley argued that Milligan was not entitled to a share as she was prevented from asserting a claim because of the illegal purpose. She relied on the equitable maxim 'He who comes to equity must come with clean hands.' A majority in the House of Lords held that Milligan was entitled to claim a share in the property.

**Key Law**

The equitable maxim prevents a plaintiff asserting an equitable title to property only if he had to rely on his illegal conduct to establish his/her claim. In this case the resulting trust arose automatically because of the contributions of Milligan.

**Key Judgment**

**Lord Browne-Wilkinson:** 'More than 100 years have elapsed since the fusion of the administration of law and equity. The reality of the matter is that, in 1993, English law has one single law of property made up of legal and equitable interests....'

## 1.2 Equitable maxims

### 1.2.1 Delay defeats equity

#### (HC) Leaf v International Galleries [1950] 2 KB 86

**Key Facts**

A contract for the sale of a painting, innocently represented as painted by Constable could not be set aside after the plaintiff had delayed in bringing an action for five years.

#### (CA) Allcard v Skinner (1887) LR 36 Ch D 145

**Key Facts**

The claimant sought to rescind gifts of her property which she had made to a religious order on the basis of undue influence. The court held that she could not do so because of her delay in bringing the action.

**Key Law**

In cases of undue influence, actions must be brought within a reasonable time after the removal of the influence.

#### (HC) Nelson v Rye [1996] 2 All ER 186

**Key Facts**

A musician tried to claim an account of earnings which had been wrongfully retained by his manager in breach of fiduciary duty. Six years elapsed before the action was brought and the court held that the equitable doctrine of laches applied and this prevented him from gaining a remedy.

## 1.2.2 He who comes to equity must do equity

(CA) Chappell v Times Newspapers Ltd [1975] 1 WLR 482

**Key Facts**

Employees who had been on strike sought an injunction to restrain their dismissal. The court refused to grant an injunction because the employees refused to sign an undertaking not to become involved in the future in strike action.

## 1.2.3 He who comes to equity must come with clean hands

(HL) Tinsley v Milligan [1993] (above)

**Key Comment**

The maxim did not prevent the claimant Milligan from successfully claiming a share since her claim was not founded on the illegality. Lord Goff dissented, arguing unsuccessfully that the maxim should apply even where the illegality was not relied on since the whole transaction was tainted with illegality. His view was rejected.

(HC) Argyll (Duchess) v Argyll (Duke) [1967] Ch 302

**Key Facts**

The Duke of Argyll claimed that his wife was barred from claiming an injunction preventing him from publishing confidential material because her adultery had caused their divorce. The court held that this was no bar to the relief claimed since it was not directly related to her claim.

**Key Law**

The general conduct of a claimant is not relevant. The maxim will only apply where the conduct has 'an immediate and necessary relation to the equity sued for'.

## 1.2.4 Equity will not allow a statute to be used as an instrument of fraud

### (CA) Bannister v Bannister [1948] 2 All ER 133

**Key Facts**

Mrs Bannister sold two cottages to her brother-in-law at undervalue on an oral undertaking that she would be allowed to live in one of the cottages rent-free for the rest of her life. Later he tried to evict her. At common law the promise was not enforceable because it had not been recorded in writing according to s 40 LPA 1925 (now s 2 LP(MP) Act 1989). The court upheld her right to remain in the cottage on the basis of the maxim that equity would not allow the statute to be used as an instrument of fraud.

## 1.2.5 Equity looks to intent rather than the form

### (CA) Tulk v Moxhay (1848) 18 LJ Ch 83

**Key Facts**

A purchaser of a plot of land covenanted with the vendor that he would 'keep the plot uncovered by buildings'. The purpose of the covenant was to ensure that there would be no building on the plot but it was drafted in positive form. It was held that the intent behind this covenant was negative.

## 1.2.6 Equity acts *in personam*

### (HC) Webb v Webb [1994] QB 696

**Key Facts**

A father purchased a flat in the name of his son in Antibes. The father intended that he would acquire an interest in equity in the property but the son refused to transfer rights to him. The father successfully brought a personal action against his son although it was to pursue a claim for real property.

**Key Law**

Rights in equity are enforced by personal order against the defendant, usually the trustee. The claimant may also have proprietary rights in the trust property.

# 2

# The Trust

**Characteristics of a Trust**

***Westdeutsche Landesbank Girozentrale v Islington BC (1996)***
Equity operates on the conscience of the owner of the legal estate. A trust must have identifiable trust property and once established the beneficiary has a proprietary interest

***Re Bowden (1936)***
Once a valid trust has been created and is fully constituted the settlor loses all rights in the trust property

**The Trust**

**Uses of a Trust**

***Barclays Bank v Quistclose Investments (1970)***
Where money is lent for an express purpose it will be held on resulting trust if that purpose is not carried out.

***Re Kayford (1975)***
Money paid in advance for goods ordered from a mail order company was held in trust for the customers

## 2.1 Characteristics of a trust

HL

### Westdeutsche Landesbank Girozentrale v Islington LBC [1996] AC 669

**Key Judgment**
**Lord Browne-Wilkinson:**

1. Equity operates on the conscience of the owner of the legal interst. In the case of a trust, the conscience of the legal owner requires him to carry out the purposes for which the property was vested in him (express or implied trust) or which the law imposes on him by reason of his unconscionable conduct (constructive trust).

2. He cannot be trustee of the property if and so long as he is ignorant of the facts alleged to affect his conscience;
3. In order to establish a trust there must be identifiable trust property;
4. Once a trust is established as from the date of its establishment the beneficiary has, in equity, a proprietary interest in the trust property, which will be enforceable in equity against any subsequent holder of the property.

See **Chapter 10** for a full analysis of the facts of *Westdeutsche*.

### (HC) Re Bowden [1936] Ch 71

**Key Facts**

The settlor transferred all her property to a trust before becoming a nun. Later when she decided to return to her former life she tried to recover her property. It was held that it could not be recovered.

**Key Law**

Once a valid trust has been created the settlor loses all rights in the property and it is irrecoverable.

## 2.2 Uses of trusts

### (HL) Barclays Bank v Quistclose Investments Ltd [1970] AC 567

**Key Facts**

Quistclose lent money to Rolls Razor, a firm in severe financial difficulties, in order to pay out dividends which had been declared on its shares. Before the dividend had been declared Rolls Razor went into liquidation. Quistclose claimed that the money lent was held on trust for them, and since the express purpose was not carried out then it should be returned to them in full. Barclays Bank claimed that the money was part of the assets of the firm.

It was held unanimously that the money was held on resulting trust for Quistclose.

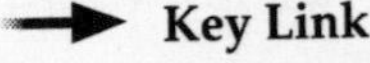

**Key Link**

See **5.2 Certainty of intention**. There was some doubt as to whether Quistclose had the intention that the money lent to Rolls Razor should be held on trust but the courts found that there was an express trust.

## HC Re Kayford [1975] 1 WLR 279

**Key Facts**

Customers ordered goods from a mail order company and sent cheques in advance. These were paid into a separate account. The company went into liquidation and the issue before the courts was whether the sums in the account belonged to the customers or the liquidator. It was held that the sums were held on trust for the customers who had paid but had not received their goods.

# 3

# *Trusts and Powers*

## The difference between a Trust and a Power

***Brown v Higgs (1803)***
The law recognises a trust and a power and also a third category which is a power which has the nature and qualities of a trust and allows the court to order division if the donee of a power has not appointed during his/her lifetime

## Powers of Appointment

***Burrough v Philcox (1840)***
Where a donee of a power dies without making an appointment a general intention in favour of the class can sometimes be presumed

***Re Weekes (1897)***
Where there is no indication that a trust will arise if a donee of a power dies without making an appointment then the property will result back to the settlor's estate

## Trusts and Powers

## The difference between Mere Powers, Hybrid Powers and Fiduciary Powers

***Re Hay's Settlement Trusts (1982)***
The duties of a donor of a mere power are: to consider periodically whether to exercise the power; consider the range of objects; consider whether individual appointments are appropriate

***Re Manisty's Settlement (1973)***
A hybrid power allows the donee of the power to appoint anyone except a defined class of persons

***Mettoy Pensions Ltd v Evans (1990)***
In some circumstances a court may be able to exercise a fiduciary power

## Exercise of Powers of Appointment

***Re Dick (1953)***
An appointment in favour of a non-object will be regarded as an excessive use of a power and will be set aside by a court

***Re Wills Trusts Deeds (1964)***
A donee can release a mere power of appointment if he/she complies with the correct formalities

***Re Mills, Mills v Lawrence (1930)***
A release of a power giving the donee absolute rights in the property will be upheld if this complies with the settlor's wishes

## 3.1 The difference between a trust and a power

HL Brown v Higgs (1803) 8 Ves 561

**Key Judgment**

**Lord Eldon:** 'There are not only a mere trust and a mere power, but there is also known to this court a power, which the party to whom it is given, is entrusted and required to execute: and with regard to that species of power the court considers it as partaking so much of the nature and qualities of a trust, that if the person who has that duty imposed on him does not discharge it, the court will, to a certain extent, discharge the duty.'

## 3.2 Powers of appointment

HC Burrough v Philcox (1840) 5 Myl & Cr 72

**Key Facts**

A testator transferred his property on trust to his two children. He included a provision that the survivor of the two children should have the power by will 'to dispose of all my real and personal estates amongst my nephews and nieces, or to as many of them as my surviving child shall think proper.'

Both children died without an appointment having been made by the survivor.

**Key Law**

It was held that the class should take in equal shares as a trust had been created which took effect on the death of the surviving child.

**Key Judgment**

**Lord Cottenham:** 'Where there appears a general intention in favour of a class, and a particular intention in favour of individuals of a class to be selected by another person, and the particular intention fails from that selection not having been made, the court will carry into effect the general intention in favour of the class.'

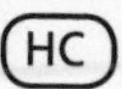

## Re Weekes [1897] 1 Ch 289

**Key Facts**

A testatrix transferred all her property to her husband giving him a life interest and also power 'to dispose of all such property by will amongst our children'. He died without making a will and therefore without exercising the power of appointment in favour of the children. The children claimed that a trust took effect on their father's death and the property was held on implied trust for them in equal shares.

**Key Law**

The husband had a mere power of appointment. There was no indication that the wife had intended the power to be in the nature of a trust. The property resulted back to the estate of the testatrix.

**Key Judgment**

**Romer J:** 'I should gather from the terms of the will that it was a mere power that was conferred on the husband, and not one coupled with a trust that he was bound to exercise. I see no words in the will to justify me in holding that the testatrix intended that the children should take if her husband did not exercise the power.'

**Key Problem**

If we compare the two cases, *Burrough v Philcox* and *Re Weekes*, it is difficult to see why they were decided differently. They were decided on the construction of the words of the gift. The gift in *Burrough v Philcox* was construed as showing an intention to benefit the objects in the event of no appointment being made, but no such intention was shown in *Re Weekes*. The dividing line between these two cases is very thin.

Other indicators that a mere power exists are:

(i) there is a gift over in default of appointment which suggests that the settlor has provided for the possibility of no appointment being made.

(ii) if the class of objects of the power is very large then the court is unlikely to conclude that there is a trust in their favour if no appointment has been made.

## (HL) McPhail v Doulton [1971] AC 424

**Key Facts**

A settlement was executed by Mr Baden in favour of a large class of persons who were employees of Matthew Hall & Co or were connected with the employees in some way. They included officers and employees or ex-officers or ex-employees of the company as well as 'any of their relatives or dependants of any such persons in such amounts at such times and on such conditions … as they think fit.' One of the issues before the court was whether this created a mere power or a trust power.

**Key Law**

Both the High Court and the Court of Appeal held that a mere power had been created, but the House of Lords held that a trust power had been created.

**Key Judgment**

**Lord Wilberforce:** 'I would venture to amplify this by saying that the court, if called upon to execute the trust power, will do so in the manner best calculated to give effect to the settlor's intentions. It may do so by appointing new trustees, or by authorising or directing representative persons of the classes of beneficiaries to prepare a scheme of distribution, or even should the proper basis for distribution appear by itself directing the trustees so to distribute…'

**Key Comment**

Today the right in this case would automatically be considered as under a discretionary trust rather than a power in the nature of a trust. There would be no doubt the words used imposed a trust rather than a power.

# 3.3 Bare or mere powers

## 3.3.1 Difference between mere powers and fiduciary powers

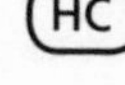 Re Hay's Settlement Trusts [1982] 1 WLR 202

**Key Facts**

Two trustees of a settlement made by Lady Hay held a power of appointment over the property subject to the trust. It was held that as they were trustees they held this power in a fiduciary capacity.

**Key Judgment**

**Megarry VC:** 'The duties of a trustee which are specific to a mere power seem to be threefold. Apart from the obvious duty of obeying the trust instrument, and in particular of making no appointment that is not authorised by it, the trustee must:

1. consider periodically whether or not he should exercise the power;
2. consider the range of objects of the power; and
3. consider the appropriateness of individual appointments.'

**Key Comment**

The main difference between the donee of a mere power and a donee of a fiduciary power is that the donee of a fiduciary power owes duties to the objects. A donee of a mere power owes no duties to the objects. They have one cause of action against the donee and that is if the power is exercised in favour of a non-object.

## 3.3.2 Hybrid and special powers

### (HC) Re Manisty's Settlement [1973] 3 WLR 341

**Key Facts**

The trustees of a settlement were given additional powers to add to a class of beneficiaries which excluded the settlor, his wife and certain named persons. The court held that the power was a hybrid power. This allowed the donees of the power to appoint anyone except a defined class of persons.

**Key Comment**

This type of power contrasts with a special power in which the donee can only exercise the power in favour of a class of named persons. A special power was granted in both *Re Weekes Settlement Trust* and *Burrough v Philcox* (see above).

## 3.4 Fiduciary powers

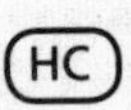

### Mettoy Pensions Trustees Ltd v Evans [1990] 1 WLR 1587

**Key Facts**

Mettoy and Co, a company which produced toys, suffered financial difficulties and went into liquidation. At the time their employees' pension scheme had an outstanding surplus of over £9 million. The trustees of the fund asked the court for directions on distributing the fund. Under the scheme the company held a power of appointment over any surplus in the fund which could be exercised in favour of the employees. If the power was not exercised the surplus would pass to the company assets. The company could no longer exercise the power because it was in liquidation. The court held it was a fiduciary power, which the court could exercise.

**Key Law**

In some circumstances the court can step in to exercise a fiduciary power. There were special circumstances in this case because the company was unable to exercise the power when it was in liquidation. The power then passed to the liquidators who represented the company, but there was a conflict because the liquidator is under a duty to act on behalf of the creditors and this would conflict with their duty to give consideration to the pensioners. Therefore the judge held that the court could exercise the fiduciary power.

**Key Link**

Compare the position of the court in a discretionary trust. The court held in *McPhail v Doulton* that it could step in and compel the trustees of a discretionary trust to exercise their powers. See **3.2** above.

## 3.5 Exercise of powers of appointment

### 3.5.1 Excessive use of a power

CA Re Dick [1953] Ch 343

**Key Facts**

A donee held a power of appointment over property left in trust for her brothers and sisters and their issue. She exercised it in favour of a sister by will but also executed a formal memorandum requiring the sister to provide part of the sum for a non-object. Although the memorandum was not regarded as a trust the Court of Appeal held that this was an excessive use of the power. The purpose of the memorandum was to benefit the non-object.

### 3.5.2 Capriciousness

HC Re Manisty's Settlement (1973) (above)

**Key Facts**

A special power of appointment, i.e. one where the settlor has specified that the power should only be exercised in favour of a class of people will be invalid if it is capricious in nature even if it is sufficiently certain. Capriciousness is not necessarily because the power is very wide but it applies if there is no sensible intention behind why a particular group has been chosen by the donor.

**Key Judgment**

**Templeman J:** [']A trust in favour of the residents of Greater London would be void on grounds of capriciousness[']

## 3.6 The release of a power

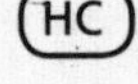

### Re Wills Trusts Deeds [1964] Ch 219

**Key Facts**

Property was held on trust on terms that the trustees had the power to appoint such of the issue of the testator or charitable institutions as the trustees should appoint. The trustees wished to release that part of the power in favour of the testator's issue so that the trust would be for exclusively charitable objects. Without such release it could not be charitable at all because a non-object could potentially benefit.

It was held that such a release was possible because in this case the trust instrument authorised release.

**Key Law**

A donee can release a mere power where he is under no obligation to exercise or to consider exercising it unless there is a gift over in default of appointment. The correct formalities must be complied with by the donee. If the donee is under a fiduciary power then he/she is not entitled to release it so as to defeat the trust unless there is authority in the trust instrument to do so.

**Key Judgment**

**Buckley J:** 'Where a power is conferred on trustees *virtute officii* in relation to their trust property, they cannot release it or bind themselves not to exercise it … The same is true if the power is conferred on persons who are in fact trustees of the settlement but is conferred on them by name and not by reference to their office, if on the true view of the facts they were selected as donees of the power because they were the trustees.'

### 3.6.1 Release of a power of appointment

CA Re Mills, Mills v Lawrence [1930] 1 Ch 654

**Key Facts**

A testator created a trust in his will directing all statutory accumulations to be held for 'such persons of a specific class which included the testator's father's children that his brother should appoint' and in default of appointment for his brother absolutely. After making several appointments the brother released the power by deed and so became absolutely entitled. This release was upheld by the court.

# 4

# Discretionary Trusts and Protective Trusts

## The nature of a Protective Trust

***Re T's Settlement Trusts (1964)***
A protective trust will be imposed by a court where it is for the benefit of the beneficiary

***Re Baring's Settlement Trusts (1940)***
Disregard of a court order could constitute a determining event.

***Re Balfour's Settlement Trusts (1938)***
Once a beneficiary's interest has determined it will revert back to the trustees and cannot be claimed by his/her trustee in bankruptcy.

## The nature of a Discretionary Trust

***Re Gestetner's Settlement (1953)***
A discretionary trust did not arise where the trustees had a mere power to appoint amongst a class of objects

***Mettoy Pension Trustees Ltd v Evans (1991)***
A discretionary trust arises where the trustee is under a duty to make a selection from a group of people but has complete discretion in choosing who is to benefit and the size of each share

## Types of Discretionary Trust

***Re Locker's Settlement Trusts (1977)***
An exhaustive discretionary trust arises where the trustees are under a duty to apply the income of a trust. They have no right to accumulate the income

***Re Gourju's Will Trusts (1943)***
Where no appointment is made by the trustees of an exhaustive discretionary there is forfeiture and protective trusts come into effect

***McPhail v Doulton (1971)***
In a non-exhaustive discretionary trust the trustees are able to accumulate the income once they have made a conscious decision not to distribute it that year

## Certainty of Objects in a Discretionary Trust

***IRC v Broadway Cottages Trust (1955)***
Traditionally the test for certainty of objects in a discretionary trust was the complete list. This no longer applies today

***McPhail v Doulton (1971)***
A discretionary trust will be valid if it can be said with certainty that any given individual 'is or is not' a member of the class

## The nature of a Beneficiary's Interest under a Discretionary Trust

***Re Smith (1928)***
The beneficiaries of a discretionary trust had sufficient interest to combine together to bring the trust to an end

***Gartside v IRC (1968)***
A beneficiary in a discretionary trust does not have sufficient interest in order to be taxed

> **Administrative unworkability**
>
> ***Re Manisty's Settlement (1973)***
> A power will not be uncertain merely because the pool of objects is wide but it may be capricious if there is no motive why a particular group has been selected by the donor
>
> ***R v District Auditor No 3 Audit District of West Yorkshire Metropolitan County Council (1986)***
> A discretionary trust may fail for administrative unworkability if the class is too large because unlike a power the court may have to step in to administer the trust

# 4.1 The nature of a protective trust

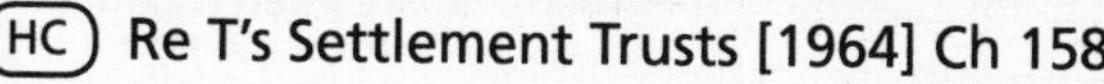

## (HC) Re T's Settlement Trusts [1964] Ch 158

**Key Facts**

A beneficiary had an interest in a trust on attaining her majority. She was immature and irresponsible and the trustees sought an order allowing them to vary the terms so that the trust became a protected life interest. The court held that although this was not strictly within the court's powers, because it was not obviously for her benefit in its own right, an order would be made postponing the vesting of the capital until a specified age and holding the property on protective trusts.

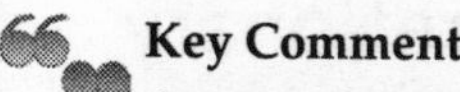

**Key Comment**

A protective trust can be used as a way to protect a beneficiary who is likely to dissipate the fund. The beneficiary of a protective trust receives a life interest in the property, which is determinable in the event of a certain event such as bankruptcy. When the trust has determined a discretionary trust will arise and the beneficiary of the protective trust becomes just one of the class of beneficiaries entitled under the discretionary trust.

## 4.1.1 What are determining events?

## (HC) Re Baring's Settlement Trusts [1940] Ch 737

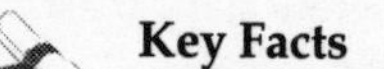

**Key Facts**

A mother disobeyed a court order which required her to return her children to the jurisdiction and a sequestration order was made by the court requiring her to give up some of her assets. The court held that this was a determining event, although in this case it was only temporary.

## Re Balfour's Settlement Trusts [1938] Ch 928

**Key Facts**

Trustees of a settlement, in breach of trust had advanced capital to a beneficiary, at his request, who was only entitled to income under a settlement. They then retained part of the income in order to make good the breach. Later the beneficiary went bankrupt and the trustee in bankruptcy claimed the life interest.

**Key Law**

The beneficiary's interest had determined when the trustees became entitled to the income of the trust. The life interest could not be claimed by the trustee in bankruptcy.

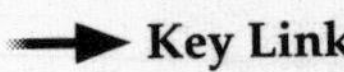

**Key Link**

See *Re Gourju* [1943] (below), where the determining event was the fact that the life tenant was no longer able to receive the income because she was living in occupied France during the Second World War.

# 4.2 Discretionary trusts

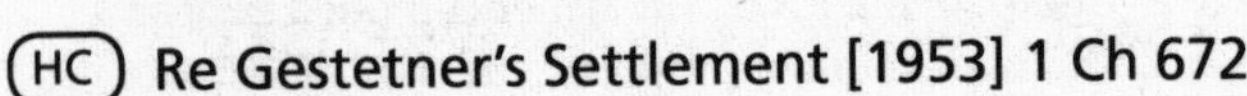

## 4.2.1 The nature of a discretionary trust

## Re Gestetner's Settlement [1953] 1 Ch 672

**Key Facts**

A settlement consisted of a capital fund to be held upon trust for such members of a specified class as the trustees might appoint with a gift over in default of appointment. The class included a large group of individuals, including descendants of the settlor's father or his uncle Jacob and any spouse, widow or widower of any such person and also five charitable bodies. The court held that this created a power of appointment and not a discretionary trust.

**Key Law**

The trustees did not have a duty to select the beneficiaries from the class of objects, but they did have a duty to consider whether to distribute the fund or not.

**Key Judgment**

**Harman J:** 'The document on its face shows that there is no obligation on the trustees to do more than consider from time to time, I suppose – the merits of such persons of the specified class as known to them and, if they think fit, to give them something.'

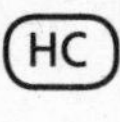

### Mettoy Pension Trustees Ltd v Evans [1991] (see facts above, Chap 3)

**Key Judgment**

**Warner J:** '… cases where someone, usually but not necessarily the trustee, is under a duty to select from among a class of beneficiaries those who are to receive income or capital of the trust property.'

### McPhail v Doulton [1971] (see facts above, Chap 3)

**Key Facts**

It was held by the House of Lords that a discretionary trust had been created in this case. The trustees had a duty to act and had no right to refuse to carry out the trust, but they had complete discretion in choosing who was to benefit, and the size of their share.

## 4.2.2 Types of discretionary trusts

### Exhaustive discretionary trusts

### Re Locker's Settlement Trusts [1977] 1 WLR 1323

**Key Facts**

The terms of a trust of an exhaustive discretionary trust required the trustees to pay, divide and apply the income for charitable purposes or among the class of beneficiaries as the trustees 'shall in their discretion determine'. The trustees did not distribute for a period between 1965 and 1968. The court held that the surplus fund should be distributed and could not be accumulated.

**Key Law**

The court can intervene in an exhaustive discretionary trust and either appoint new trustees where the trustees have failed to distribute or direct the trustees to distribute. In an exhaustive discretionary trust the trustees are under a duty to distribute and have no discretion whether or not to act.

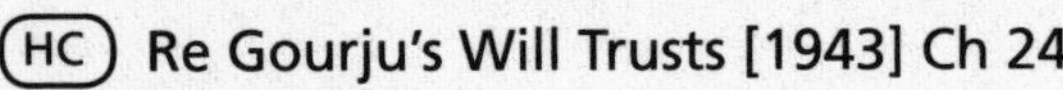

## Re Gourju's Will Trusts [1943] Ch 24

**Key Facts**

The main beneficiary of a trust was temporarily unable to receive the income of the trust because she was living in Nice in France which became enemy occupied territory in the Second World War. This was an exhaustive discretionary trust so the trustees had no power to accumulate the income and instead this caused forfeiture and protective trusts came into effect allowing the income to become payable to one or more members of the class of beneficiaries.

**Key Comment**

An exhaustive discretionary trust arises where the trustees have no express power to retain all or part of the income from the fund.

### Non-exhaustive discretionary trusts

## (HL) McPhail v Doulton [1971] (above, Chap 3)

**Key Comment**

In this case the trustees were able to accumulate the income and were under no duty to make a distribution every year. However, they were under a duty to consider whether or not to distribute or to accumulate the income each year.

# 4.2.3 The nature of a beneficiary's interest in a discretionary trust

## (HC) Re Smith [1928] Ch 915

**Key Facts**

Property was held on a discretionary trust for a mother and her three children. The court held that the beneficiaries in a discretionary trust had sufficient interest in the trust to combine together and claim the legal title.

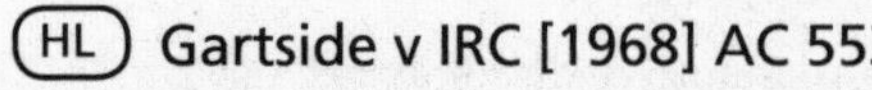

## Gartside v IRC [1968] AC 553

**Key Facts**

A non-exhaustive discretionary trust had been created in favour of Mr Gartside, his wife and their children. No distribution had been made at the date of Mr Gartside's death and the IRC sought estate duty on the fund arguing that he had sufficient interest to be taxed.

**Key Law**

The court held that Mr Gartside's estate was not subject to tax. His interest in the fund only arose when an appointment was made in his favour.

**Key Judgment**

**Lord Wilberforce:** 'No doubt in a certain sense a beneficiary under a discretionary trust has an "interest". The nature of it may sufficiently for this purpose be spelt out by saying that he has a right to be considered as a potential recipient of benefit by the trustees and a right to have his interest protected by a court of equity ... But that does not mean that he has an interest which is capable of being taxed by reference to its extent in the trust's income...'.

**Key Problem**

What do the beneficiaries of a discretionary trust own? In *Gartside v IRC* it was held that there was no group interest which could be split between the beneficiaries. The court concluded that two or more persons cannot have an individual right unless they hold it jointly or in common.

**Key Comment**

There is a conflict between *Re Smith* and *Gartside v IRC*. The view in *Gartside v IRC* is favoured today so the beneficiaries of a discretionary trust cannot be said to own the fund as a group. There are taxation provisions which allow them to be taxed in other ways. The view of the court in *Gartside v IRC* has been applied to subsequent cases of exhaustive discretionary trusts such as *Re Weir's Settlement Trusts* [1969] 1 Ch 657 and *Sainsbury v IRC* [1970] Ch 712.

## 4.2.4 Certainty of objects in discretionary trusts

### The old test for certainty in discretionary trusts

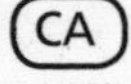


**IRC v Broadway Cottages Trust [1955] Ch 20**

**Key Facts**

The traditional approach to certainty of objects was that a discretionary trust where all the beneficiaries could not be completely ascertained would be void for uncertainty. This is no longer the law today.

### The new test for certainty of objects in a discretionary trust

**McPhail v Doulton [1971] (above, Chap 3)**

**Key Facts**

The test for certainty of objects in a discretionary trust was the same test as applied to powers of appointment under *Re Gulbenkian* (see below, **Chapter 5**).

**Key Judgment**

**Lord Wilberforce:** '… the rule recently fastened upon by the courts in *IRC v Broadway Cottages Trust* ought to be discarded and the test for the validity of discretionary trusts ought to be similar to that accepted by this House in *Re Gulbenkian's Settlement Trusts* [1970] for powers, namely that the trust is valid if it can be said with certainty that any given individual "is or is not" a member of the class.'

The case was remitted back to the Chancery Division where Brightman J and later three judges of the Court of Appeal reconsidered the facts of the case. In the Court of Appeal all three judges took different approaches.

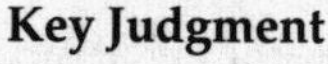

**Key Judgment**

**Stamp LJ** adopted a strict approach to the question of certainty. He held that although the trustees were no under a duty to draw up a complete list of beneficiaries they had to be able to survey the range and … 'validity would depend on whether it was possible to say with any certainty of any individual "is or is not a member of a class for only this can you make a survey of the range of objects."' On this basis he would have found the trust in this case void for uncertainty because he thought the term 'relations' was conceptually uncertain but he followed previous decisions which held that 'relations' meant 'next of kin' and following the majority held that the trust was valid.

**Key Judgment**

**Megaw LJ** adopted a less strict view and held that the test was satisfied if it was possible to say of a substantial number of beneficiaries that they fell within the class. He distinguished 'conceptual' and 'evidential' certainty and held that the test was satisfied provided the class was conceptually certain.

**Key Judgment**

**Sachs LJ** agreed with Megaw LJ and held that the court in deciding on the issue of certainty in a discretionary trust would never be defeated by evidential uncertainty. On the facts of the case of *McPhail v Doulton* the terms 'relatives' and 'dependants' were conceptually certain and therefore the trust was not void for uncertainty.

## 4.2.5 Administrative unworkability in a power of appointment and discretionary trust

### Administrative unworkability in a power of appointment

HC Re Manisty's Settlement [1973] (above, Chap 3)

**Key Judgment**

**Templeman J:** 'In my judgment … the mere width of a power cannot make it impossible for trustees to perform their duty nor prevent the court from determining whether the trustees are in breach … I conclude that a power cannot be uncertain merely because it is wide in ambit…'.

### Administrative unworkability in a discretionary trust

DC **R v District Auditor No 3 Audit District of West Yorkshire MCC ex p West Yorkshire MCC [1986] RVR 24**

**Key Facts**

A county council which was about to be abolished by the government held a surplus of over £400,000 in their accounts. They tried to create a discretionary trust on the following terms: '… for the purposes of benefiting "any or all or some of the inhabitants" of West Yorkshire for a number of purposes including assisting their economic development within the county, providing assistance for youth, ethnic and minority groups…'. The inhabitants of West Yorkshire numbered about 2.5 million people.

The court held that although the class was conceptually certain, the range of objects made such a gift administratively unworkable and void.

**Key Judgment**

**Lloyd LJ:** 'A trust with as many as two and a half million potential beneficiaries is, in my judgment, quite simply unworkable. The class is far too large … My conclusion is that the dictum of Lord Wilberforce in *McPhail v Doulton* remains of high persuasive authority despite *Re Manisty*. Manisty's case was concerned with a power, where a function of the court is more restricted. In the case of a trust, the court may have to execute the trust. Not so in the case of a power.'

# 5

# The Three Certainties

**Definition of Certainty**
***Knight v Knight (1840)***
A trust can only exist if the words are imperative; the subject matter is certain and the objects of the trust are certain

## The Three Certainties

### Certainty of Objects

**Fixed trusts**
***IRC v Broadway Cottages Trust (1954)***
A trustee must be able to draw up a complete list of all the beneficiaries
**Discretionary Trusts**
***McPhail v Doulton (1971)***
The trustee must be able to say whether a single beneficiary 'is or is not' within the class
**Gifts subject to a condition precedent**
***Re Barlow's Will Trusts (1979)***
The test for certainty of objects in a gift subject to a condition precedent is whether one person comes within the class
**A fixed trust can only be upheld if it has conceptual and evidential certainty**
***Re Gulbenkian's settlement (1970)***
**Missing beneficiaries**
***Re Benjamin (1902)***
A Benjamin order protects a trustee from an action for breach of trust if the proceeds of an estate are distributed and one or more of the beneficiaries are missing
**Resolving uncertainty by appointing a third party**
***Re Tuck's Settlement Trusts (1978)***

### Certainty of Intention

***Jones v Lock (1865)***
Loose conversation does not show the intention to create a trust
***Paul v Constance (1977)***
Intention to create a trust can be shown without using the word trust so long as there is intention to be bound
***Re Kayford (1975)***
***Barclays Bank v Quistclose (1970)***
**Precatory words**
***Re Adams and Kensington Vestry (1884)***
***Re Steele's Will Trusts (1948)***
Precatory words may create a trust if intention was shown from surrounding circumstances
***Comiskey v Bowring-Hanbury (1905)***
Precatory words do not show intention to create a trust
***Midland Bank v Wyatt (1995)***
If the intention is a sham there is no trust
***Staden v Jones (2008)***
On the creation of a trust it was not necessary to use the word trustee
***Re Farepack etc (2008)***
Moneys in an account expressly intended to be kept in trust could be claimed by customers after a company went into administration

### Certainty of Subject Matter

***Palmer v Simmonds (1854)***
A gift of the bulk of an estate will fail for uncertainty of subject matter
***Sprange v Barnard (1789)***
A gift of the remaining part of an estate failed for uncertainty of subject matter
***Re London Wine Co (Shippers) (1986)***
***Re Goldcorp (1995)***
Unsegregated tangible assets could not form the subject matter of a trust
***Hunter v Moss (1994)***
Unsegregated intangible assets (shares) were capable of forming the subject matter of a trust
***Anthony v Donges (1998)***
A trust of an unspecified part of an estate will be void for uncertainty
***Re Golay (1965)***
A reasonable income could be sufficiently certain
***Boyce v Boyce (1849)***
A gift dependent on selection by another beneficiary will be void
***MacJordan Construction Ltd v Brookmount (1992)***
No trust created of a builders' retainer held as percentage of a general fund

## 5.1 General introduction

CA Knight v Knight (1840) 3 Beav 148

**Key Judgment**

**Lord Langdale MR:** 'First, if the words were so used, that upon the whole, they ought to be construed as imperative; secondly, if the subject of the recommendation or wish be certain; and thirdly, if the objects of persons intended to have the benefit of the recommendation or wish be also certain.'

## 5.2 Certainty of intention

### 5.2.1 Was sufficient certainty of intention shown?

CA Jones v Lock (1865) LR 1 Ch App 25

**Key Facts**

Robert Jones, responding to criticism that he had not given his child a gift, placed a cheque for £900 in the hand of the baby, aged nine months. He said 'I give this to baby and I am going to put this away for him.' He took the cheque away and put it into his safe. A few days later he died. The issue before the courts was whether the cheque was held on trust for the son or whether it could be claimed by the residuary legatees under the will.

The court held that there had been no declaration of trust.

**Key Judgment**

**Lord Cranworth LC:** 'The case turns on the very short question whether Jones intended to make a declaration that he held the property in trust for the child; and I cannot come to any other conclusion than that he did not. I think it would be a very dangerous example if loose conversations of this sort, in important transactions of this kind, should have the effect of declarations of trust.'

## Paul v Constance [1977] 1 WLR 527

**Key Facts**

Mr Constance and Ms Paul lived together as man and wife. Mr C received a sum in compensation for an industrial injury and he put the money in a deposit account in his own name. He told Ms Paul on a number of occasions that the money in the account was as much hers as it was his. Later joint winnings from bingo were paid into the account and a subsequent withdrawal was regarded as a withdrawal of joint money. After his death Ms P claimed the fund from the administratrix Mrs Constance, his surviving wife.

It was held that Mr C had declared himself to be trustee of the fund by his words and by his actions, and so 50 per cent of the fund was held for Ms P.

**Key Law**

The evidence for the necessary intention to create a trust was gathered from Mr C's assurance that 'the money is as much yours as mine', although at no time did he use the word trust.

**Key Link**

Consider the two cases below as examples of the uses of the trust today. See **Chapter 2**.

## Staden v Jones [2008] 2 FLR 1931

**Key Facts**

The Court of Appeal emphasised that on the creation of a trust it was not necessary to refer expressly to the word 'trustee', but according to Arden LJ the words said or acts done by the settlor must have been intended to have had that meaning.

**Key Link**

See cases on the constitution of a trust. See **Chapter 7**.

## HC Re Farepak Foods and Gifts Ltd (in administration) [2008] 2 BCLC 1

**Key Facts**

A court will accept conduct as sufficient evidence of intention to create a trust. Farepack operated a Christmas savings scheme where customers were able to save for Christmas over a year. The money received from the customers was not kept in a separate account. When the company went into liquidation they were unable to claim that their money was held in trust. However the court did decide money deposited by customers three days before the company went into liquidation was held on trust because the company had executed a deed that the money belonging to the customers was to be put into a separate account.

## HC Re Kayford [1975] (above, Chap 2)

**Key Facts**

Customers of a mail order company had paid in advance for goods and they claimed this money was held on trust when the company went into liquidation.

**Key Law**

It was held that there was a trust for the customers based on the intention of the company when the moneys were paid into a separate account. As a result, the trustee in bankruptcy could not claim the money in that account on behalf of the creditors.

## HL Barclay's Bank v Quistclose Investments Ltd [1970] (above, Chap 2)

**Key Facts**

Money was advanced to Rolls Razor by Quistclose Investments in order to pay dividends, but Rolls Razor went into liquidation before the dividends were paid.

**Key Law**

The House of Lords held that Quistclose had created a two-tier trust. The first trust was created when Quistclose lent the money to Rolls Razor on trust to pay the dividends. This was an express trust. When the dividends could not be paid, Rolls Razor held the money on a secondary trust for Quistclose.

The creditors of Rolls Razor had no claim to the money because it was trust money and was never owned beneficially by Rolls Razor, and it should be returned in full to the beneficiary Quistclose. There was sufficient certainty of intention because Quistclose lent the money for the sole purpose of paying the dividends.

**Key Link**

See **Chapter 10**. Rolls Razor held the fund on resulting trust for Quistclose. The money was transferred on express trust for the purpose of paying dividends when the purpose could not be carried out it resulted back to Quistclose.

## 5.2.2 Precatory words

Precatory words are words such as 'hope' or 'wish'. They do not generally create a trust and the fund can be kept absolutely by the recipient.

### CA Re Adams and Kensington Vestry (1884) 27 Ch D 394

**Key Facts**

A testator left property on the following terms: 'unto and to the absolute use of my wife Harriet, in full confidence that she will do what is right as to the disposal thereof between my children either in her lifetime or by will after her decease.'

It was held that the words did not create a trust and the wife was able to claim the property absolutely for herself.

### HL Comiskey and Others v Bowring-Hanbury and Another [1905] AC 84

**Key Facts**

The testator left his property to his wife in full confidence that '… at her death she will devise it to such one or more of my nieces as she may think fit'. He added a gift over in default of appointment. A majority in the House of Lords held that the testator's will created a gift to his wife during her life but subject to a trust over the remaining part in favour of the surviving nieces to be shared in accordance with the wife's will or otherwise equally. This was in spite of the use of the words 'in full confidence'.

**Key Law**

If the will as a whole and surrounding circumstances are sufficiently clear for the court to conclude that a trust was intended by the testator, then a trust will be found in spite of the use of precatory words. If there is evidence that the testator intended a trust to arise but the precatory words used were based on words from an earlier trust instrument, the court may also conclude that there is a trust.

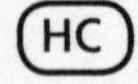

### Re Steele's Will Trusts [1948] Ch 603

**Key Facts**

A testatrix left a diamond necklace to her son by will. The will contained the following clause: 'I request the said son to do all in his power by his will or otherwise to give effect to this my wish'. The words had been included because the testatrix wanted her son to make the necklace a family heirloom. The words used appeared to be precatory but evidence was given that the form of words had been expressly taken from another earlier case where a trust had been created. This indicated that there was an intention to create a trust.

## 5.2.3 'Sham' intention

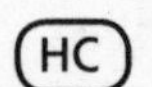

### Midland Bank plc v Wyatt [1995] 1 FLR 696

**Key Facts**

A husband and wife executed a declaration of trust over the jointly owned family home, in favour of the wife and daughters. The document was put into a safe but was not acted on. The couple continued to act as joint owners of the property. When the husband's business failed, the bank successfully obtained a charging order against the house. The husband relied on the trust in order to prevent the bank from enforcing the order against the property. It was held that the purported declaration of trust in favour of the wife and children was a sham and therefore he retained the entire beneficial interest in the property.

**Key Law**

The intention to create a trust must be genuine and not a sham, so that the settlor does not really intend the trust to be acted on except in certain circumstances.

# 5.3 Certainty of subject matter

## 5.3.1 The testator must identify the subject matter clearly

### HC Palmer v Simmonds (1854) 2 Drew 221

**Key Facts**

A testatrix left the residue of her estate to a named beneficiary, subject to a provision that if he died without children, he should leave 'the bulk of his residuary estate' for the benefit of four named individuals.

It was held that there was no trust because there was no identifiable property which was capable of becoming the subject matter of a trust.

### HC Sprange v Barnard (1789) 2 Bro CC 585

**Key Facts**

A testatrix left her property to her husband with instructions that he should divide up equally the remaining part of what is left and what he did not want for his own use between her brother and sister.

**Key Law**

The law draws a distinction between unascertained property where it involves tangible goods such a personal property and intangible goods such as money and shares.

## 5.3.2 Tangible property

### HC Re London Wine Co (Shippers) Ltd [1986] PCC 121

**Key Facts**

Purchasers of wine claimed bottles of wine were held in trust for them after the suppliers went into liquidation, and could not be claimed by the trustee in bankruptcy. The wine was held in large warehouses but had not been segregated for the individual purchasers from the whole.

It was held there was no express trust for the purchasers because there was no certainty of subject matter.

**Key Judgment**

**Oliver J:** 'It seems to me that in order to create a trust it must be possible to ascertain with certainty not only what the interest of the beneficiary is to be, but to what property it is to attach…'.

### Re Goldcorp Exchange [1995] 1 AC 74

**Key Facts**

Suppliers of gold bullion went into liquidation and a number of purchasers claimed proprietary rights in the bullion, arguing it had been held in trust for them.

It was held that the bullion could not be held on trust for the purchasers, because there was no identifiable property.

**Key Law**

Only those purchasers who could show that their bullion had been segregated could claim their order in full. Until segregation the property could not be said to be held in trust because the subject matter was uncertain.

## 5.3.3 Intangible property

### Hunter v Moss [1994] 1 WLR 452

**Key Facts**

The defendant held a large shareholding and declared himself to be trustee in respect of a 5 per cent holding of the shares for the benefit of the claimant. Since the defendant held 950 shares, it represented about 50 shares. The shares had not been segregated from the whole.

It was held that a trust was created in favour of the claimant.

**Key Law**

The law treats intangible property differently from tangible property when considering whether the subject matter of a trust is certain. Intangible property such as money and shares does not have to be segregated from the whole in order for a trust to arise.

**Key Problem**

Not everyone agrees that tangible assets such as wine and intangible assets such as shares can be distinguished in this way. In particular, there will be a difference between an *inter vivos* transfer of shares and a gift on death. If a shareholder declares himself to be trustee of shares from a larger shareholding then it will not be enforceable by the beneficiary until he has divested himself of the ownership of those shares otherwise he could continue to claim them for himself.

**Key Comment**

Re London Wine was distinguished in *Hunter v Moss* because in the former case the property was tangible property and individual bottles of wine could be distinguished by year and type, whereas the shares were intangible property and no single share was distinguishable from another. It would make no difference if the shares had been segregated.

HC

### MacJordan Construction Ltd v Brookmount Brostin Ltd [1992] BCLC 350

**Key Facts**

A firm of builders claimed that a retainer of 3 per cent held by a property development company, to ensure that the work was carried out to a satisfactory standard, was held on trust for them. It had not been separated from other funds and simply amounted to a percentage of the total amount paid.

The sum was not held in trust, because the subject matter of the trust was not sufficiently identifiable and the builders could not claim any priority when the company became insolvent.

## 5.3.4 Certainty of beneficial interest

HC

### Anthony v Donges [1998] 2 FLR 775

**Key Facts**

A husband left a gift to his estranged wife: 'such minimal part of my estate of whatsoever kind and wheresoever situate save as aforesaid she may be entitled to under English law for maintenance purposes.'

The court held that this was void for uncertainty as it was impossible to ascertain what the wife was entitled to under English law for maintenance purposes.

## Re Golay and others [1965] 2 All ER 660

**Key Facts**

A testator instructed his trustees to allow the beneficiary to enjoy one of his flats during her lifetime and also to receive a 'reasonable income' from other properties.

It was held that this was sufficiently certain because the words 'reasonable income' could be construed objectively and it was possible for the court to apply this determinant.

**Key Judgment**

**Ungoed-Thomas J:** 'In this case the yardstick indicated by the testator is not what he or any other specified person subjectively considers to be reasonable but what he identifies objectively as "reasonable income". The court is constantly involved in making such objective assessments of what is reasonable and it is not to be deterred from doing so because subjective influences can never be wholly excluded …'.

## (HC) Boyce v Boyce (1849) 16 Sim 476

**Key Facts**

The settlor left two houses on trust for his two daughters. One of the daughters was required to make a selection from the two houses, and the remaining house would pass to the other daughter. When the first daughter failed to make a selection before she died, the second daughter claimed one of the houses for herself.

The trust failed for uncertainty of subject matter.

**Key Comment**

This suggests that the claim of the second sister was dependent on the claim by the first sister. It could not exist independently of the first claim.

# 5.4 Certainty of objects

**Key Facts**

A trust will only be valid if it exists for the benefit of identified legal persons. The test for certainty of objects varies according to whether it is a fixed trust or a discretionary trust, or a gift subject to a condition precedent.

## 5.4.1 Fixed trusts

### The test for certainty of objects in a fixed trust

HC **IRC v Broadway Cottages Trust [1954] 1 All ER 878**

**Key Facts**

In a fixed trust, the class must be capable of ascertainment, which means that the trustee must be able to draw up a complete list of all the beneficiaries of the trust. The trust will fail if such a list cannot for some reason be drawn up.

### Conceptual certainty

HL **Re Gulbenkian's Settlement Trusts [1970] AC 508**

**Key Facts**

A special power of appointment was granted to the trustees to appoint in favour of Nubar Gulbenkian '… and any wife and his children or remoter issue … and any person … in whose house or apartment or in whose company or under whose care or control or by or with whom [he] may from time to time be employed or residing.' There were trusts over in default of appointment. The power was upheld because it could be said with certainty whether any given individual was or was not a member of the class, so the power was valid.

**Key Law**

A trust to divide a fund equally between 'my old friends' would be void for uncertainty because the class is conceptually uncertain. No court could define what 'an old friend' means. The same problem would arise if the gift were to my 'best friends'.

**Key Judgment**

**Lord Upjohn:** '…Suppose the donor directs that a fund be divided equally between "my old friends" then unless there is some admissible evidence that the donor has given some special "dictionary meaning" to that phrase which enables the trustees to identify that class with sufficient certainty, it is plainly bad as being too uncertain…'.

→ See **4.2.4 Certainty of objects in discretionary trusts**.

## Evidential certainty

### HL Re Gulbenkian's Settlement Trusts (above)

**Key Judgment**

**Lord Upjohn:** 'If a donor directs … trustees to make … provision for "John Smith", then gives legal effect to that provision it must be possible to identify "John Smith". If the donor knows three John Smiths then by the most elementary principles of law neither the trustees nor the court in their place can give effect to that provision; neither the trustees nor the court can guess at it. It must fail for uncertainty unless of course admissible evidence is available to point to a particular John Smith as the object of the donor's bounty.'

**Key Comment**

A fixed trust will not fail if it is conceptually certain and evidentially certain even though the trustees may not be able to physically locate every beneficiary on the list. If the settlor left his estate to be divided equally between 'all my children', a 'child' is conceptually clear and the trustees may know that the settlor had five children but one went to America 10 years ago and has not been heard of since. That beneficiary is said to be unascertainable.

## Missing beneficiaries

### HC Re Benjamin [1902] 1 Ch 723

**Key Facts**

The testator left his estate to his children in equal shares. He had 12 children. All but one could be traced, but one had disappeared on holiday in France while the testator was still alive.

It was held that he could be presumed dead and his share could be shared out between the other brothers and sisters. If it turned out that he was still alive then the other beneficiaries would be liable for the return of his share and the trustee would not be liable for breach of trust.

**Key Law**

A 'Benjamin Order' allows the trustees to distribute the proceeds of an estate without fearing an action for breach of trust from a beneficiary who was presumed dead and who suddenly returns and claims a share. The order can only be made after all practicable inquiries have been made.

## Resolving uncertainty in a provision in a will

### (CA) Re Tuck's Settlement Trusts [1978] Ch 49

**Key Facts**

Sir Adolf Tuck wanted to ensure that his estate passed to those who were of and remained in the Jewish faith. He specified in his will that future descendants would only inherit his estate if they married a wife of Jewish blood who at the time of her marriage continued to worship according to the Jewish faith. In the event of a dispute, 'the decision of the Chief Rabbi in London shall be conclusive'.

**Key Law**

Uncertainty over the class of beneficiaries in a trust can be resolved by nominating someone who is qualified to resolve such an issue.

**Key Judgment**

**Eveleigh LJ:** 'Different people may have different views or be doubtful as to what is "Jewish faith" but the Chief Rabbi knows and can say what meaning he attaches to the words…'.

## 5.4.2 Discretionary trusts

### (HL) McPhail v Doulton [1971] AC 424

**Key Facts**

See **Chapters 3 and 4**.

**Key Law**

The test to be applied for certainty of objects in a discretionary trust is the same as the test for certainty of objects for a power, namely the 'given postulant test' or 'is or is not' test. Under this test it must be possible to say of any given individual that he is or is not within the class. The trustees do not need to have a complete list of all the beneficiaries before exercising their discretion.

**Key Judgment**

**Lord Wilberforce:** 'a trustee with a duty to distribute, particularly among a potentially very large class, would surely never require the preparation of a complete list of names, which anyhow would tell him little that he needs to know…'.

## (CA) McPhail v Doulton (1971) (above)

**Key Judgment**
**Sachs LJ:** '…the court is never defeated by evidential uncertainty, and it is in my judgment clear that it is conceptual certainty to which reference was made when the 'is or is not a member of the class' test was enunciated … the suggestion that such trusts could be invalid because it might be impossible to prove of a given individual that he was not in the relevant class is wholly fallacious.'

**Key Link**
**Chapter 4** considers the development of the test for certainty of objects in a discretionary trust.

# 5.4.3 Gifts subject to a condition precedent

## (CA) Re Allen [1953] Ch 810

**Key Facts**
A gift made to a family member subject to the condition that he 'shall be a member of the Church of England and an adherent to the doctrine of that Church' was upheld on the basis that, in spite of uncertainty surrounding the term 'adherent to the doctrine of the Church of England', so long as there was one person who could clearly show that he or she was within the definition it could be certain.

## (HC) Re Barlow's Will Trusts [1979] 1 WLR 278

**Key Facts**
The testatrix left a number of valuable paintings with instructions that 'any member of my family and any friends of mine' could, when she died, buy any of the paintings at the prices contained in a catalogue of valuations made five years before her death. These prices were well below the market value of the paintings.

**Key Law**

It was held that although the class of 'any friends of mine' would be conceptually uncertain, this was not a gift to a class but a series of gifts to the testatrix's friends. Therefore anyone who could prove that he/she was a friend of the testatrix could claim the right to buy a painting.

The test for certainty of objects for gifts subject to a condition precedent is whether it can be said with sufficient certainty that one person qualifies within class. The fact that there may be residual uncertainty about others will not defeat the gift. It is up to the claimant to prove that he/she comes within the class.

The *Re Allen* test was applied as discussed above.

**Key Judgment**

**Lord Browne-Wilkinson:** 'In my judgment, Lord Upjohn was considering only cases where it was necessary to establish all the members of the class. He made it clear that the reason for the rule is that in a gift which requires one to establish all the members of the class … you cannot hold the gift good in part, since the quantum of each friend's share depends on how many friends there are …'.

## 5.4.4 Administrative unworkability

### R v District Auditor No 3 Audit District of West Yorkshire MCC ex p West Yorkshire MCC [1986] (above, Chap 4)

**Key Facts**

A discretionary trust in favour of the inhabitants of the County of West Yorkshire failed because although the class was conceptually certain the range of objects which comprised over 2.5 million people was so wide as to be 'incapable of forming anything like a class'. It was thus administratively unworkable and void.

# 6

# *Formalities in the Creation of a Trust*

## Formalities in the Creation of a Trust

### Declarations of Trust *Inter Vivos*

***Rochefoucauld v Boustead (1897)***
***Bannister v Bannister (1948)***
***Hodgson v Marks (1971)***
Property will be held in trust even where the formalities of creation have not been complied with if a person knows that they are not to benefit absolutely but to hold on trust for another

### Declaration of Trust by Will

**s 9 Wills Act 1837**
A will must be made in writing, signed by the testator and witnessed by two witnesses who attest the signature

### Dispositions of subsisting equitable Interests

A subsisting equitable interest must be transferred in writing to satisfy
s 53(1)(c) LPA 1925
***Vandervell v IRC (1967)***
***Oughtred v IRC (1960)***
***Grey v IRC (1960)***
A constructive trust is outside s 53(1)(c) LPA 1925
***Neville v Wilson (1997)***
A declaration of a new trust or a variation of an existing trust is outside
s 53(1)(c)
***Re Vandervell's Trusts No 2 (1974)***
***Re Holt's Settlement (1969)***

### Declaration of a trust over land

A declaration of a trust over land must be manifested and proved by some writing under s 53(1)(b)

***Random House UK Ltd v Allason (2008)***
A defendant argued that the claimant could not claim certain land because it was held in trust for others. No trust was found as he had no written evidence to prove it.

# 6.1 Declarations of trust *inter vivos*

## 6.1.1 Trusts of land

**Key Comment**

**Section 53(1)(b) Law of Property Act 1925**: 'A declaration of trust respecting any land or any interest therein must be manifested and proved by some writing signed by some person who is able to declare such a trust or by his will.'

### Random House UK Ltd v Allason [2008] EWHC 2854

**Key Facts**

The defendant owed money to the claimant. He argued that certain land was held on trust for others and could not be used to satisfy the debt. However there was no written evidence to satisfy s 53(1)(b) LPA 1925 showing a trust had been created.

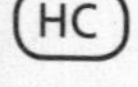


### Rochefoucauld v Boustead [1897] 1 Ch 196

**Key Facts**

Land had been sold by a mortgagee to a purchaser who had taken expressly on trust for the claimant. The claimant sought a declaration that the defendant had acquired the land on trust for her. The defendant claimed that there could be no trust because there was no written evidence in support of her claim.

**Key Law**

It was held that although the legal formalities had not been complied with, the defendant held the property on trust for the claimant.

**Key Judgment**

**Lindley LJ:** 'It is a fraud on the part of a person to whom land is conveyed as a trustee, and who knows it was so conveyed, to deny the trust and claim the land for himself.'

### Bannister v Bannister [1948] 2 All ER 133

**Key Facts**

The claimant transferred her house to her brother-in-law. He agreed orally that he would hold the property on trust for her and that she would have a life interest in the property. It was held that no express trust arose but the brother-in-law held as constructive trustee.

**Key Link**

See **1.2.4**.

### CA Hodgson v Marks [1971] Ch 892

**Key Facts**

The claimant transferred her house to her lodger but on the understanding that she would retain some interest in the property. The house was then sold to a third party. It was held that her rights were binding on the third party. Her rights arose under a constructive trust.

**Key Comment**

Compare *Rochefoucauld v Boustead* where the failure to comply with the requirements of s 53(1)(b) LPA 1925 was not fatal on the principle that a statute will not be used as an instrument of fraud, with *Bannister v Bannister and Hodgson v Marks* where the court held that s 53(1)(b) did not apply because the circumstances gave rise to a constructive trust which under s 53(2) does not require compliance with s 53(1)(b).

**Key Link**

Consider the maxims of equity in **Chapter 1**.

## 6.2 Declarations of trust by will

**Key Facts**

Under s 9 Wills Act 1837 a will must be made in writing, signed by the testator and witnessed by two witnesses who must attest the signature.

**Key Link**

Secret trusts are an exception to s 9 Wills Act 1837 because the law deems them to operate outside the Wills Act ('dehors the will'). See **9.1**.

## 6.3 Dispositions of subsisting equitable interests

**Key Comment**

The following cases all concern attempts to avoid the payment of stamp duty, which at the time was payable on deeds of gift. The tax was payable on the deed rather than the transaction. If the transaction was made orally then no tax would be paid, but it needed to satisfy s 53(1)(c) Law of Property Act to be a valid disposition, which requires a disposition of an equitable interest to be made in writing.

### HL Vandervell v IRC [1967] 2 AC 291

**Key Facts**

Mr Vandervell wanted to found a Chair in Pharmacology at the Royal College of Surgeons. He decided to do so by transferring some shares in his company, Vandervell Products, which were held by nominee trustees, to the College. He retained an option to repurchase the shares for £5,000 when the College had sufficient capital to found the chair. The College received dividends worth over £250,000. The Inland Revenue wanted to tax Vandervell on the amount. They argued that at all times Mr Vandervell retained an equitable interest in the shares because he did not comply with s 53(1)(c) Law of Property Act 1925. This section required the disposition of an equitable interest to be evidenced in writing. If it was not evidenced in writing then the disposition would be void. If both the legal interest and the equitable interest are transferred at the same time, then s 53(1)(c) does not apply.

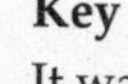

**Key Law**

It was held that as Mr Vandervell was the beneficiary of a bare trust, he did not have to comply with s 53(1)(c) and was entitled simply to direct the trustees to transfer the legal title to the trust property. There would be no separate disposition of the equitable title. Transfer of both the legal and equitable interest at the same time does not require writing.

**Key Judgment**

**Lord Upjohn:** '... when the beneficial owner owns the whole beneficial estate and is in a position to give directions to his bare trustee with regard to the legal as well as the equitable estate there can be no possible ground for invoking the section where the beneficial owner wants to deal with the legal estate as well as the equitable estate.'

## Oughtred v IRC [1960] AC 206

**Key Facts**

Mrs Oughtred owned 72,000 shares in a company and was also tenant for life in a settlement containing a large number of shares, in which her son Peter was entitled to the property in remainder. As a tax-saving device Mrs Oughtred and her son decided to transfer shareholdings, so Peter gave up his remainder in the estate to his mother and she agreed to transfer her 72,000 shares to him. A deed of release was executed. The Inland Revenue argued that stamp duty was payable, as there had been a contract for sale which would attract duty. However, as the shares were in a private company the contract could be specifically enforced. The Oughtreds argued that the equitable interest had already passed by reason of the right to specifically enforce the contract. Where a contract is specifically enforceable, a constructive trust is said to arise as soon as the contract is effective because the equitable interest passes to the purchaser.

A constructive trust is outside s 53(1)(c) and so the agreement did not need to be in writing.

The majority in the House of Lords thought that there had been a transfer of sale for the purposes of the Stamp Act, and stamp duty was payable.

**Key Judgment**

**Lord Radcliffe (dissenting judgment):** 'There was, in fact, no equity in the shares that could be asserted against her, and it was open to her, if she so wished, to let the matter rest without calling for a written assignment, from her son … It follows that … this transfer cannot be treated as a conveyance of the son's equitable reversion at all …'.

**Key Comment**

Lord Radcliffe gave a dissenting judgment in this case, arguing that ownership in equity had passed as soon as the agreement became specifically enforceable in which case there was no conveyance of interest.

## Neville v Wilson [1997] Ch 144

**Key Facts**

A number of shares were held by nominees on behalf of a company, U Ltd, on trust for J Ltd, a family company. J Ltd had been struck off the register and the shareholders of J Ltd informally agreed to liquidate the company and to divide its equitable interest in U Ltd between them proportionately to their existing shareholding. The agreement was purely oral so there was no written evidence to comply with s 53(1)(c). However the court held that the oral agreement had created a constructive trust of the shareholding and s 53(2) applied.

**Key Judgment**

**Nourse LJ:** 'The simple view of the present case is that the effect of each individual agreement was to constitute the shareholder an implied or constructive trustee for the other shareholders, so that the requirement for writing contained in s 53(1)(c) was dispensed with by s 53(2)'.

## Re Vandervell's Trusts (No 2) [1974] Ch 269

**Key Facts**

There was further litigation in relation to the interest in the shares that had resulted back to the Vandervell estate. Both the trustees of the children's settlement and the executors of the estate claimed the shares. At first instance Megarry J upheld the claim of the executors to the shares, but this was reversed by the Court of Appeal. The executors had argued that the shares could only pass to the trustees if there was a declaration in writing, but the court rejected this, saying that there was no need for a written instrument. There were several reasons for this but the most important reason was that s 53(1)(c) does not apply to the declaration of new trusts. The law would not regard this as a disposition within the section.

## (HC) Re Holt's Settlement [1969] 1 Ch 100

**Key Facts**

The terms of a trust were successfully varied to allow those entitled to the remainder a share of the income, but delaying their entitlement to capital from age 21 to 30. It was questioned whether the variation was required to be in writing according to s 53(1)(c).

**Key Law**

It was held that a variation of a trust under the Variation of Trusts Act 1958 did not require every disposition of each beneficial interest to be in writing under s 53(1)(c).

## (HL) Grey v IRC [1960] AC 1

**Key Facts**

In 1949 the settlor Mr Hunter transferred shares of nominal amounts to trustees on trust for his six grandchildren. In 1955 the settlor transferred 18,000 £1 shares to the same trustees upon trust for himself. In order to avoid paying stamp duty he orally directed his trustees to hold the property upon the trusts of the six settlements. A few weeks later, Hunter executed a declaration of trust in writing. If the interest passed on the oral instruction to the trustees, then stamp duty would not be payable, but if there was a transfer when the declaration of trust was put in writing, then that would attract tax. The House of Lords held that the transfer of the equitable interest only took place when the written document was executed, and the oral instructions by Hunter to the trustees were ineffective and no interest passed.

# 7

# Constitution of Trusts

### Transfer of Property to Trustees

***Choithram (T) International SA v Pagarani (2001)***
Where trust property was vested in only one of a number of trustees this would be sufficient to constitute a trust

### Mode of transfer necessary for a completely Constituted Trust

**Land**
***Richards v Delbridge (1874)***
An assignment of an interest in land must be made by deed
**Shares**
***Milroy v Lord (1862)***
Legal title to shares passes when they have been registered in the name of the transferee
**Chattels**
***Thomas v Times Books (1966)***
Title to a chattel passes when there is a clear intention to give and the property is delivered

### Transfer of property requiring an act of a third party to perfect the title

***Re Rose (1952)***
***Mascall v Mascall (1985)***
A transfer will be complete in equity when the transferor has done everything in his power to transfer the legal title to the transferee

### Unconscion-ability

***Pennington v Waine (2002)***
Even where there are still steps for the transferor to complete a transfer will be upheld if it would be unconscionable for him/her to revoke the transfer

### Constitution by receipt of trust property in another capacity

***Re Ralli's Will Trusts (1964)***
A trust may be fully constituted where the trustee receives trust property in some other capacity e.g. as executor of the settlor

### Declaration of self as trustee

***Jones v Lock (1865)***
***Paul v Constance (1977)***
***Re Vandervell (No 2) (1974)***

### Effect of a completely constituted trust

***Staden v Jones (2008)***
A beneficiary can enforce his/her share once a trust has been completely constituted

**Enforcing incompletely constituted trusts**

***Pullan v Koe (1913)***
***Cannon v Hartley (1949)***
A beneficiary may be able to enforce an incompletely constituted trust if he/she has given consideration
***Re Cook's Settlement Trusts (1965)***
***Re Plumptre's Marriage Settlement (1910)***
A beneficiary who has failed to give consideration cannot enforce an incompletely constituted trust
***Fletcher v Fletcher (1844)***
A beneficiary may be able to enforce a trust of a promise to create a trust

**Exceptions to the rule that 'equity will not assist a volunteer'**

***Strong v Bird (1874)***
An imperfect gift or the release of a debt may be perfected where a donee is appointed an executor or administrator of the donor's estate if a continuing intention to release the debt or make a gift until death can be shown
***Re Gonin (1979)***
An imperfect gift cannot be upheld where there is no evidence of a continuing intention to give on the death of the donor

***Donatio Mortis Causa***

A gift made in the contemplation or expectation of immediate death will be upheld even if the formalities are not strictly complied with
***Wilkes v Allington (1931)***
Death from an alternative cause will not prevent a donatio mortis causa arising
***Sen v Headley (1991)***
***Re Lillingston (1952)***
***Birch v Treasury Solicitor (1951)***
***Woodard v Woodard (1991)***
There must be delivery or symbolic delivery of the subject matter
***Cain v Moon (1896)***
***Re Craven (1937)***

# 7.1 The constitution of an express trust

## (HC) Milroy v Lord (1862) 31 LJ Ch 798

**Key Judgment**

**Turner LJ:** '…in order to render a voluntary settlement valid and effectual, the settlor must have done everything which, according to the nature of the property comprised in the settlement was necessary to be done in order to transfer the property ..he may do this if he transfers the property to a trustee… or declares that he himself holds it in trust for those purposes…but in order to render the settlement binding, one or other of these modes must … be resorted to.'

# 7.2. Transfer of property to trustees

## Choithram (T) International SA v Pagarani [2001] 2 All ER 492

**Key Facts**

A very wealthy man from the British Virgin Islands wished to set up a charitable foundation, to which he intended to transfer most of his property including company shares. He became gravely ill, but before he died he signed a trust deed establishing the foundation. There were to be seven trustees including himself and after he signed the deed he stated that he was giving all his wealth to the foundation. His health deteriorated further and he died before he had formally transferred the property to the foundation.

The claimants were the man's first wife and her children who argued that the gifts he had made to the foundation were ineffective because of a failure of transfer. Both the trial judge and the Court of Appeal in the British Virgin Isles found that a trust had been created in spite of the failure of the settlor to vest the properties in the foundation. On appeal to the Privy Council by the defendants, who were the executors of the settlor, it was also held that there was a completely constituted trust.

**Key Judgment**

**Lord Browne-Wilkinson:** 'The foundation has no legal existence apart from the trust declared by the foundation trust deed. Therefore the words "I give to the foundation" can only mean "I give to the trustees of the foundation trust deed to be held by them on the trusts of the foundation trust deed." Although the words are apparently words of outright gift they are essentially words of gift on trust…'.

**Key Comment**

The trust property was only vested in one of the trustees, but once the property was vested in one trustee this would be sufficient to constitute the trust.

The court held that there could be no distinction between the case where one of the trustees simply declared himself as sole trustee and a case where the donor declares himself to be one of the trustees. The court were anxious to uphold the gift on the principle of unconscionability. (See the later case of *Pennington v Waine*, 7.1.5 below.)

# 7.3 Mode of transfer necessary for a completely constituted trust

## 7.3.1 Land

CA Richards v Delbridge (1874) LR 18 Eq 11

**Key Facts**

A grandfather intended to create a trust of some leasehold property to his grandson. He assigned it in writing to the boy's mother. An assignment of a lease must be made by deed, so the trust was incompletely constituted and the transfer failed.

## 7.3.2 Shares

CA Milroy v Lord (above)

**Key Facts**

An attempt was made to create a trust consisting of 50 shares in the Bank of Louisiana in favour of the claimant by transferring them on trust to Lord. The Bank required that the shares be registered in the name of the transferee at the Bank for title to pass. This was never done although a deed of assignment had been executed and the share certificates had been delivered.

Although the transferor had intended to create a trust no trust had been created because the trust was incompletely constituted.

## 7.3.3 Chattels

### (HC) Thomas v Times Books [1966] 1 WLR 911

**Key Facts**

The widow of Dylan Thomas claimed ownership of the manuscript of his play *Under Milk Wood* from a third party. He had received it from the author in a taxi during a night of heavy drinking. It was held that the property had passed and the wife could not claim the property back.

**Key Law**

Where chattels are the subject matter of a trust or a gift evidence of an intention to give and delivery of the subject matter of the gift or trust will fully constitute the trust or perfect the gift.

## 7.3.4 Transfer of property requiring an act of a third party to perfect the title

### (CA) Re Rose [1952] Ch 499

**Key Facts**

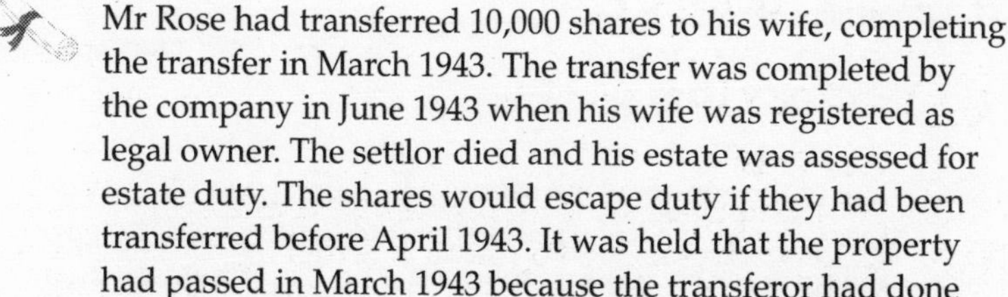

Mr Rose had transferred 10,000 shares to his wife, completing the transfer in March 1943. The transfer was completed by the company in June 1943 when his wife was registered as legal owner. The settlor died and his estate was assessed for estate duty. The shares would escape duty if they had been transferred before April 1943. It was held that the property had passed in March 1943 because the transferor had done everything in his power to transfer the shares and the final act was one that had to be carried out by a third party.

## CA Mascall v Mascall (1985) 49 P & CR 119

**Key Facts**

A father wanted to transfer property to his son. He executed a transfer of the house to his son and handed over the land certificate. Before the son had registered his title at the Land Registry, the son and father argued and the father sought to have the transfer set aside. It was held that the father had done all that was necessary for him to do, and the transfer was complete.

**Key Law**

A transfer will be complete in equity when the transferor has done everything in his power to transfer the legal title to the transferee.

**Key Comment**

Both *Re Rose* and *Mascall v Mascall* concerned absolute transfers of property, but the principles also apply to the constitution of a trust and the transfer of property to trustees.

# 7.3.5 Unconscionability

## CA Pennington v Waine [2002] 1 WLR 2075

**Key Facts**

Ada Crampton owned a 75 per cent shareholding in a private company of which she was one of the directors. She told her nephew that she was giving him 400 of her shares and that she wanted him to become a director. She repeated this to one of the company's auditors. She signed a stock transfer form, but instead of transferring it to her nephew she gave the form to the auditors who put it on file. When she died, the form was still with the auditors and she had not made any provision for the 400 shares in her will. The court decided that although she had not done everything that was necessary to be done under Re Rose, the transfer could still be upheld on the principle of unconscionability. She had told him that she was transferring the shares to him and that she wanted him to become a director, and he could not do this without a shareholding of his own.

**Key Law**

The court may uphold a transfer even where there are further steps to be carried out by the transferor, where it would be unconscionable for the transferor to revoke the transfer.

## 7.3.6 Constitution by receipt of trust property in another capacity

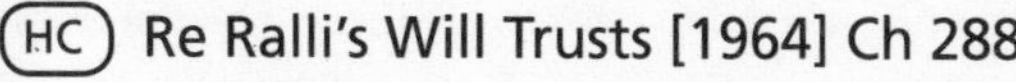

### (HC) Re Ralli's Will Trusts [1964] Ch 288

**Key Facts**

A testator left property on trust for his widow for life and remainder for his two daughters. One daughter, H, had promised as part of a marriage settlement that she would settle after-acquired property in favour of volunteers. She died before her mother but had not transferred her interest under the trust to the marriage settlement. Her executor was trustee of H's marriage settlement as well as her mother's will.

The court held that as he was trustee of both the trust and the marriage settlement, the property within the trust came to him in his capacity as trustee of the settlement and so the trust was fully constituted.

**Key Law**

A trust may be fully constituted where the trustee receives trust property in some other capacity in purely fortuitous circumstances.

# 7.4 Declaration of self as trustee

### (CA) Jones v Lock (1865) (above, Chap 5)

**Key Facts**

The court held that he had not created a trust of the property as he did not show sufficient intention to create a trust. Alternatively the cheque had not been properly transferred as an outright gift to the baby because it had not been endorsed on the back.

### (CA) Paul v Constance (1977) (above, Chap 5)

**Key Facts**

Money was placed in a deposit account in the name of Mr Constance. He told Ms Paul on many occasions that the money was as much hers as his. This was sufficient declaration of trust although the specific moment when the trust was declared was not clear.

**Key Link**

Consider the intention necessary in order to create an express trust; see **Chapter 5**.

### (CA) Re Vandervell's Trusts (No 2) (1974) (above, Chap 6)

**Key Facts**

When shares transferred by Mr Vandervell to the Royal College of Pharmacology resulted back to his estate, the question was whether or not there had been a declaration of trust in favour of his children. The court inferred such a declaration from circumstances and the actions of the trustees.

**Key Link**

Consider *Vandervell v IRC* for the facts of the initial transfer; see **Chapter 6**.

## 7.5 Effect of a completely constituted trust

### (CA) Staden v Jones [2008] 2 FLR 1931

**Key Facts**

Under an agreement drawn up by a husband and wife on their separation in 1971 the husband agreed to leave half his estate to their daughter if the wife would convey her share of the matrimonial home to the husband immediately. The wife transferred her share. The husband later remarried and transferred the house into joint names of himself and his new wife. On his death the property passed under the rules of survivorship to his new wife. The daughter claimed that she had a half-share held under trust.

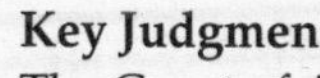

**Key Judgment**

The Court of Appeal, overturning the decision at first instance, found in favour of the daughter, holding that there was a fully constituted trust of a half-share in the house at the time of her parent's separation which was enforceable.

# 7.6 Enforcing incompletely constituted trusts: covenants and promises to create a settlement

## 7.6.1 Beneficiaries who are deemed to have given consideration

### (HC) Pullan v Koe [1913] 1 Ch 9

**Key Facts**

A wife covenanted to settle after-acquired property in excess of £100. She received the sum of £285 but did not settle this sum as agreed, and paid it into a separate account. The children were able to enforce her promise as they were parties to the marriage settlement and were not volunteers, as they were deemed to have given consideration.

### (HC) Cannon v Hartley [1949] Ch 213

**Key Facts**

A daughter was able to sue on a deed of separation which had been drawn up between her parents and herself when her father did not pay her an agreed sum of money received from his parents. Although she was a volunteer she had the right to claim damages for breach of the covenant to settle property because she was a party to the deed of separation.

## 7.6.2 Beneficiaries who have failed to give consideration

### HC Re Cook's Settlement Trusts [1965] Ch 902

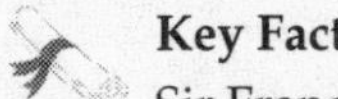

**Key Facts**

Sir Francis Cook covenanted that he would settle the proceeds of sale of certain property, including a valuable painting, on trust for his family. He gave this to his wife and the court considered whether the beneficiaries could enforce the covenant in relation to the proceeds of sale of this picture. It was held that the beneficiaries were volunteers and could not enforce an incompletely constituted trust and recover the painting from his wife.

### HC Re Plumptre's Marriage Settlement [1910] 1 Ch 609

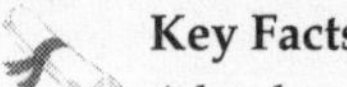

**Key Facts**

A husband and wife had agreed to settle any property they received exceeding £500 and to pay the income to any issue, and if there were none to the wife's next of kin. The wife did not pay the agreed sums and the next of kin sought to enforce the covenant, as there were no children to the marriage. They were not entitled to enforce.

**Key Law**

The beneficiaries of a covenant to settle after-acquired property within a marriage settlement could not force the parties to the covenant to settle property because they had not provided consideration.

## 7.6.3 Trusts of the benefit of a covenant

### HC Fletcher v Fletcher (1844) 4 Hare 67

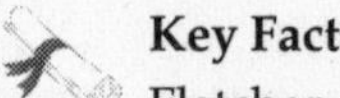

**Key Facts**

Fletcher covenanted with trustees that if either or both of his illegitimate sons Jacob and John should survive him and attain the age of 21, his executors would pay to the covenantees £60,000 within 12 months of his death to be held on trust for the relevant natural issue. Jacob survived and he sued the executor's of his father's estate. It was held that he had the right to sue because the trustees held the benefit of the covenant on trust for him.

**Key Comment**

The important point about this case is that the court found that the benefit of the covenant formed the subject matter of a trust. So the claimant based the claim not on the covenant itself, but on a trust of the covenant. However there is some doubt about the validity of this approach since a trust requires intention, and there is no evidence that Fletcher intended to create a trust of the benefit of the covenant.

## 7.7 Exceptions to the rule that 'equity will not assist a volunteer'

### 7.7.1 The rule in *Strong v Bird*

Strong v Bird (1874) LR 18 Eq 315

**Key Facts**

The defendant's stepmother lived in his house and paid him for her board and lodging. The stepson owed her £1100 and they agreed that she would pay a reduced amount to cover the loan. After two quarters she resumed paying at the full amount, and she told him she did not want the debt repaid. She should have put this into writing if she wanted to formally release him from the debt. She died some years later, appointing her stepson as executor.

**Key Law**

It was held that his appointment perfected the imperfect release of the debt, and the stepson was not required to repay the sum to the estate.

There are several conditions that must first be satisfied for the rule to apply:

1. the donor must have intended to make an *inter vivos* gift or release a debt;
2. the intention must continue until the date of death;
3. the donee must have been appointed an executor or an administrator must have been appointed.

### HC Re Gonin [1979] Ch 16

**Key Facts**

A mother wanted to give her house to her daughter, but she wrongly thought that the daughter could not inherit the house because she was illegitimate. Instead she wrote the daughter a cheque for £33,000, which was found after the mother's death. The daughter could not cash the cheque, as a personal cheque cannot be cashed after death. The daughter was administratrix of her mother's estate and claimed the house under the rule in *Strong v Bird*. It was held that she could not claim the house, because the mother did not show a continuing intention to benefit the daughter up until her death. Once she signed the cheque, she no longer intended the daughter to have her house.

**Key Law**

The rule in *Strong v Bird* will only apply if there is a continuing intention to benefit the claimant until death.

## 7.7.2 *Donatio mortis causa*

### HC Cain v Moon [1896] 2 QB 283

**Key Law**

There are three essentials for a valid *donatio mortis causa*:

1. The gift must have been made in contemplation, though not necessarily in the expectation of death.
2. The subject matter of the gift must have been delivered to the donee.
3. The gift must have been made under such circumstances as to show that the property is to revert to the donor if he should recover.

### Contemplation of death

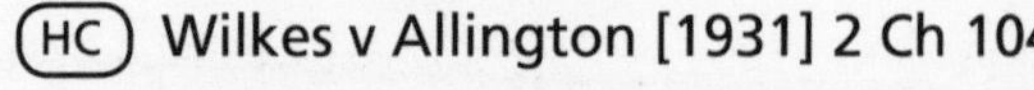

### HC Wilkes v Allington [1931] 2 Ch 104

**Key Facts**

The donor had been diagnosed with cancer and as a consequence he made a number of incomplete gifts. He later caught pneumonia and died. It was held that he had made a valid *donatio mortis causa*.

**Key Law**

A *donatio mortis causa* may still be valid even though the donor has contemplated death from one cause but died from another.

### There must be delivery of the subject matter of the gift

### CA Sen v Headley [1991] Ch 425

**Key Facts**

The claimant had lived for many years with the deceased, but they never married. On his deathbed in hospital he said to her that the house and contents were hers. The title to the house was unregistered and he gave her a key to a box where the deeds were kept. She had a set of house keys and he kept a set for himself. It was held that the transfer of the key to the strong box containing the title deeds was sufficient delivery.

Land can be the subject matter of a *donatio mortis causa*, and in unregistered land, transfer of the title deeds is evidence of delivery.

**Key Comment**

It is difficult to see how there can be delivery in registered land today, since under the LRA 2002 land certificates are no longer issued on registration of title at the Land Registry.

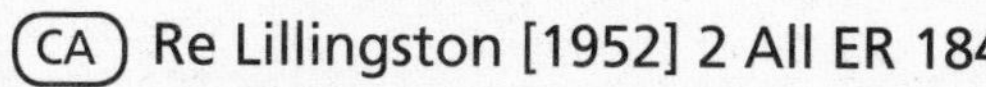

### CA Re Lillingston [1952] 2 All ER 184

**Key Facts**

The donor gave to the donee a key to a trunk which itself contained another key to a safe deposit box and that also contained another key to another safe deposit box. There was a valid *donatio mortis causa* of the contents of each safe deposit box and also of the trunk. The transfer of the first key was sufficient delivery.

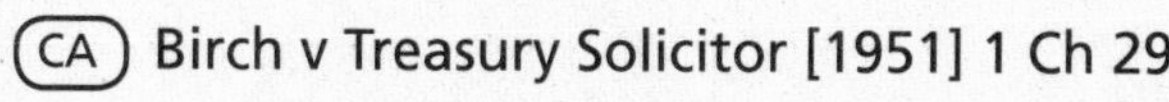

### CA Birch v Treasury Solicitor [1951] 1 Ch 298

**Key Facts**

Before going into hospital Mrs Birch, who was seriously ill, told her nephew and his wife that she wanted them to have the money she had in three separate accounts and her post office account and she gave them the passbooks. Delivery of the passbooks was sufficient evidence of a *donatio mortis causa* because the books had to be produced in order to withdraw funds from any of the accounts.

## Woodard v Woodard, The Times, 18th March, 1991

### Key Facts

A son claimed the right to sell a car given to him by his late father. The father, who had become seriously ill, had given him a set of keys to the car but had retained a set for himself. The court held that there was no outright gift but there was evidence to support a valid *donatio mortis causa*.

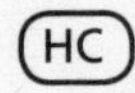

## Re Craven's Estate [1937] 1 Ch 423

### Key Judgment

Farwell J in an obiter judgment suggested that the retention of a second set of keys to property by the donor may be inconsistent with an intention to part with the property, although the claimant may be able to prove otherwise as in *Woodard v Woodard* (**above**).

# 8

# *Private Purpose Trusts*

***Morice v Bishop of Durham (1805)***
Every trust must have a definite object. There must be somebody in whose favour the court can decree specific performance
***Re Astor's Settlement Trusts (1952)***

## Exceptions to the beneficiary principle: the anomalous exceptions

In all cases the gift must comply with the perpetuity principle and must comply with the certainty rule
**Tombs and monuments:** ***Mussett v Bingle (1876)***; ***Re Endacott (1960)***; ***Re Hooper (1932)***
**Animals:** ***Pettingall v Pettingall (1842)***; ***Re Dean(1889)***
**Others:** Masses for the dead ***Re Hetherington (1990)*** (upheld as charitable); ***Bourne v Keane [1919]*** (upheld as non-charitable)

## Exceptions to the beneficiary purpose: capricious purposes

A purpose trust within the anomalous exceptions will not be upheld if the purpose is capricious
***Brown v Burdett (1882)***
***M'Caig v University of Glasgow (1907)***
***M'Caig's Trustees v Kirk Session of United Free Church of Lismore (1915)***

## Exceptions to the beneficiary principle: Re *Denley (1969)*

Where a trust is expressed for a purpose it will still be upheld if it is for the benefit of individuals with sufficient interest to enforce

Charitable gifts are an exception to the rule requiring a trust to have a beneficiary to enforce. This is because the A-G can enforce any charitable trust (see **Chapter 11**)

### Unincorporated Associations

***Conservative and Unionist Central Office v Burrell (1982)***
An unincorporated association has a number of key characteristics including a common purpose where people are bound by mutual undertakings and rules identifying who has control over the body and the terms on which such control is exercisable and the body can be joined at will
***Neville Estates v Madden (1962)***
Gifts to unincorporated associations can either be gifts to the members as joint tenants or a gift to members subject to their rights and liabilities (***Re Recher's Will Trusts (1972)***) or as a gift held in trust for all present and future members
***Re Lipinski's Wills Trusts (1976)***
A gift held for the members subject to the rules of membership could be used for any purpose within the club's rules even if a purpose had been specified by the testator
***Re Grant's Wills Trusts (1980)***
A gift to a club which did not have power to dissolve itself could not be upheld under the principle in ***Re Recher's Will Trusts (supra)***
***Hanchett-Stamford v A-G (2009)***

# 8.1 The beneficiary principle

## (CA) Morice v Bishop of Durham (1805) 10 Ves Jr 522

**Sir William Grant:** 'Every trust must have a definite object. There must be somebody in whose favour the court can decree specific performance.'

## (HC) Re Astor's Settlement Trusts [1952] Ch 534

**Key Facts**

The terms of a trust made by Viscount Astor were '… that the income was to be applied for the maintenance of good understanding between nations' and '… the preservation of the independence and integrity of the newspapers'. These purposes were not charitable. The trust could not be upheld as a private purpose trust because:

(i) it offended against the beneficiary principle and
(ii) the objects of the trust were uncertain.

# 8.2 The exceptions to the beneficiary principle

## 8.2.1 Tombs and monuments

### (HC) Mussett v Bingle [1876] WN 170

**Key Facts**

This is a strange case about a testator who wished his wife's first husband to be remembered in a special memorial, which he agreed to pay for. A gift of £300 to erect a monument was upheld as an exception to the purpose trust cases but a second gift for the upkeep of the monuments failed, being void for perpetuity. No limit had been placed on the length of time the trust was to last.

### (CA) Re Endacott [1960] Ch 232

**Key Facts**

Money was left by Albert Endacott to the North Tawton Parish Council 'for the purpose of providing some useful memorial to myself '. The gift failed because it offended the beneficiary principle and did not come within any of the exceptions, because it was unclear what was meant by some useful memorial.

**Key Law**

A purpose trust within the exceptional cases will fail if it is too vague in its terms or it does not comply with the perpetuity period.

### (HC) Re Hooper [1932] 1 Ch 38

**Key Facts**

A sum of money was left for the purpose of the upkeep and care of certain family graves and monuments as well as a tablet in a window in the church for as long as the trustees could legally do so. This was upheld for a period of 21 years.

**Key Comment**

Even where a purpose trust is upheld within the exceptional cases, it must still comply with the perpetuity period.

## 8.2.2 Animals

HC Pettingall v Pettingall (1842) 11 LJ Ch 176

**Key Facts**

A gift by the testator of £50 per annum for the upkeep of his favourite mare was upheld.

HC Re Dean (1889) 41 Ch D 552

**Key Facts**

A gift of £750 per annum for 50 years was left by William Dean to his trustees for the upkeep of his eight horses and his hounds. The judge held that this was a valid private purpose trust.

**Key Law**

The court upheld the gift, although it offended the perpetuity period. The case can be justified on the basis that the judge considered lives as including the life of an animal. However, later cases have held that lives must be human lives.

## 8.2.3 Trusts for saying masses for the dead

HC Re Hetherington [1990] Ch 1

**Key Factss**

In this case the saying of masses was held in public and so could be a valid charitable trust as it satisfied the public benefit test.

**Key Comment**

However, it was held in *Bourne v Keen* [1919] AC 815 that the saying of masses for the dead will still be valid as a private purpose trust if it is held in private.

## 8.2.4 Capricious purposes

HC Brown v Burdett (1882) 21 Ch D 667

**Key Facts**

The testator left a house to trustees, instructing them to block up most of the rooms for a period of 20 years, and then the house was to pass to a named person. It was held that the gift could not be upheld.

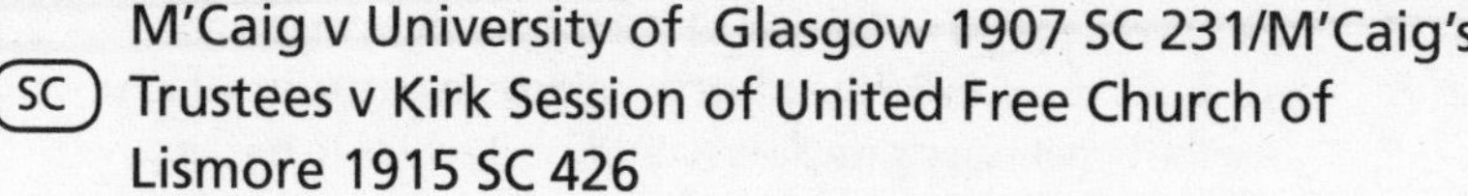

## M'Caig v University of Glasgow 1907 SC 231/M'Caig's Trustees v Kirk Session of United Free Church of Lismore 1915 SC 426

**Key Facts**

In the first case a trust was set up for the purpose of erecting statues of the testator and 'artistic towers' around his estate. The second case concerned a similar trust to erect bronze statues of the testatrix's parents and their children. Both trusts were set aside on public policy grounds. The judge described them as a 'sheer waste of money'.

**Key Comment**

The court appears to have been interfering with a testator's complete freedom to deal in his property as he wishes after his death subject to certain statutory controls such as the Inheritance (Provision for Family and Dependants) Act 1975.

**Note** that changes to the perpetuity period made by the Perpetuities and Accumulations Act 2009 do not affect non-charitable purpose trusts.

# 8.3 The approach in Re Denley

## Re Denley's Trust Deed [1969] 1 Ch 373

**Key Facts**

Land was transferred by Charles Denley to trustees with the purpose of providing a sports field for employees of his company. The transfer was limited for a period of 21 years. There were no named beneficiaries so it appeared to fail under the beneficiary principle. The court held that although the trust appeared to be expressed for a purpose it was for the benefit of individuals and so it did not offend the beneficiary principle because they had sufficient interest to enforce.

**Key Judgment**

**Goff J:** 'I think there may be a purpose or object trust, the carrying out of which would benefit an individual or individuals, where the benefit is so indirect or intangible or which is otherwise so framed as not to give this person any *locus standi* to apply to the court to enforce the trust, in which cases the beneficiary principle would, as it seems to me, apply to invalidate the trust, quite apart from any question of uncertainty or perpetuity. Such cases can be considered if and when they arise. The present is not, in my judgment of that character…'.

**Key Problem**

*Re Denley* raises problems because it is difficult to decide whether it was upheld as a purpose trust or as a private purpose trust. The wording of the trust was for the use of recreation facilities of employees so it was a non-charitable purpose trust. However Goff J suggests that as there were ascertainable beneficiaries it could be upheld. The difficult problem is that in a conventional private trust a beneficiary will own an equitable interest, but in this trust the employees merely had a right to use the land for a limited period of time. They did not have an interest in the land.

# 8.4 Unincorporated associations

## 8.4.1 The definition of an unincorporated association

### Conservative and Unionist Central Office v Burrell [1982] 1 WLR 522

**Key Facts**

The case concerned the status in law of the Conservative Association. The Inland Revenue wanted to assess it for corporation tax, which was only payable if it was an unincorporated association. It was held that it was not an unincorporated association because it lacked some of the key characteristics. In particular, the people joining the party did not have a set of mutual rights and duties arising from a contract between them and there were no rules determining who controlled the body and its funds. The local branches of the Conservative Party had these rules, but not Central Office.

**Key Law**

1. An unincorporated association is composed of two or more people bound together for a common purpose,
2. The people are bound by mutual undertakings arising from a contract between them,
3. The body has rules which identify (a) who controls the body and its funds and (b) the terms on which such control is exercisable,
4. The body can be joined at will.

## 8.4.2 Constructions of gifts to unincorporated associations

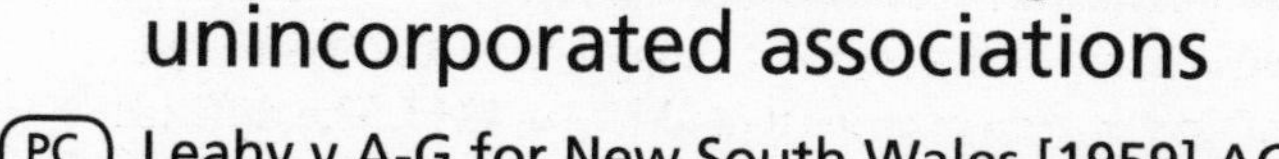

### PC Leahy v A-G for New South Wales [1959] AC 457

**Key Facts**

A testator left land of over 730 acres to be held on trust 'for such an order of nuns of the Catholic Church or the Christian Brothers as my executors and trustees shall select'. The gift failed as a charitable trust because some orders are purely contemplative whose activities were not recognised as charitable purposes in law. It also failed as a private trust. If it were held to be a gift for the purposes of the group then it would fail for perpetuity and it would fail as a gift to the members to enjoy jointly as the numbers of all the orders were too extensive to enforce this for their benefit.

**Key Comment**

The gift in *Leahy v New South Wales* was upheld under a special statute passed by the New South Wales government permitting it to have charitable status even though contemplative orders could benefit.

### HC Neville Estates v Madden [1962] Ch 832

**Key Facts**

Cross J held that gifts to the members of an unincorporated association fell into three categories:

1. A gift to members at the relevant date as joint tenants, each having the right to sever a share;
2. A gift subject to the contractual rights and liabilities of the members towards each other. There would be no right to sever a share and a member's interest will on his death or resignation

accrue to the remaining members;

3. A gift to present or future members which will fail unless it is expressly within the perpetuity period.

## The contract holding theory

(HC) **Re Recher's Will Trusts [1972] Ch 526**

**Key Facts**

Funds left to the London and Provincial Anti-Vivisection Society were held for the Society as part of its assets and would be owned by the members according to the rules of the Society.

**Key Law**

On the facts of the case the gift failed because the Society had been dissolved before the date of the gift.

**Key Judgment**

**Brightman J:** '… The legacy in the present case to the London & Provincial Society ought to be construed as a legacy of that type, that is to say, a legacy to the members beneficially as an accretion to the funds subject to the contract which they had made *inter se*.'

(HL) **Re Lipinski's Wills Trusts [1976] Ch 235**

**Key Facts**

Harry Lipinski left his residuary estate to an association called the Hull Judaeans (Maccabi) Association, an unincorporated association 'in memory of my late wife to be used solely in the work of constructing new buildings for the association and/or improvements to the said buildings'. The next of kin challenged the gift, arguing that it was invalid because it was a gift for a purpose and the purpose could last indefinitely so making it void for perpetuity.

**Key Law**

It was held that the gift could be construed as a gift to the members and it would be possible for the members to use it for any purpose according to their rules. If it was a gift for a purpose it could still be upheld because the purpose was one that could be carried out immediately and under *Re Denley* there were specific beneficiaries who could enforce.

## (HC) Re Grant's Wills Trusts [1980] 1 WLR 360

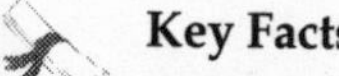

**Key Facts**

A gift was made to the Chertsey Labour Party. The nature of the Labour Party was such that a local branch of the Labour Party could not be an unincorporated association because it did not have its own rules, the local branches of the Labour Party do not have separate rules, therefore the gift failed.

**Key Link**

Consider what happens to surplus assets on the dissolution of an unincorporated association. See **10.2.3**.

## (HC) Hanchett-Stamford v Attorney-General [2009] Ch 173

**Key Facts**

Lewison J applied the contract holding theory which holds that the fund is owned by the members according to their contract. However where there is a sole surviving member of an unincorporated association all remaining funds could be claimed by the surviving member.

## (HC) Re Horley Town FC [2006] EWHC 2386

**Key Facts**

Members of this football club ranged from full to associate and temporary members. The trustees applied to the court to ask how different types of membership may effect distribution of the funds. Lawrence Collins J concluded that where membership prevented a member from deciding on whether the club should be wound up or not, in this case the associate and temporary members should not have a right to a share in the funds if the club was wound up.

# 9

# Secret Trusts and Mutual Wills

***McCormack v Grogan (1869)***
The basis of secret trusts was originally the prevention of fraud. If a testator tells the secret trustee that a trust is to be established then it would be a fraud on the part of the trustee to deny it.

## The fully secret trust

***Ottaway v Norman (1972)***
A fully secret trust must satisfy THREE requirements: intention; communication any time up until the death of the testator and acceptance by the secret trustee

***Re Snowden (1979)***
A secret trust will only arise if the words used impose a trust rather than a moral obligation (intention)

***Wallgrave v Tebbs (1855)***
A letter found amongst papers after the testator's death is not proper communication of a secret trust to a secret trustee

***Re Stead (1900)***
Where secret trustees hold the trust property as joint tenants communication of the trust to one of the joint tenants will be sufficient

***Re Boyes (1884)***
There is no communication if there is a suggestion that communication will be made after the execution of the will and it is not made until after the death of the testator

***Re Cooper (1939)***
Where a codicil adds further property to the trust then this too must be communicated to the secret trustee

***Moss v Cooper (1861)***
Silence can constitute acceptance of a secret trust by a secret trustee

## Secret Trusts

### The half-secret trust

***Blackwell v Blackwell (1929)***
A half-secret trust must satisfy THREE requirements: intention, communication before or at the time of execution and acceptance

***Re Keen (1937)***
There will be sufficient communication where the testator hands a sealed envelope to the trustee containing the names of the beneficiaries if the settlor shows that he intends to create a trust

***Re Rees Wills Trust (1950)***
Trustees of a half-secret trust are unable to keep payments promised to them where a will imposes a trust over the whole sum

### Issues arising from secret trusts

***Re Gardner (No 2) (1923)***
The estate of a beneficiary who predeceased the testator could keep the gift promised in the secret trust although it is usually regarded as taking effect only on the death of the testator

***Re Young (1951)***
A witness to a will could still claim a gift under a secret trust contained in the will in spite of the operation of s 15 Wills Act 1837 because the gift takes effect outside the will

### Mutual Wills

***Re Oldham (1925)***
Identical wills will only take effect as mutual wills where the gifts were intended to take effect as mutual wills

***Re Dale (1994)***
The consideration for a mutual will is the fact that the first party had executed a will but not taken advantage of his/her right to change it at any time before death

***Goodchild v Goodchild (1997)***
Strong evidence that the parties did not intend to be bound by a mutual will e.g. from a solicitor
***Olins v Walters (2009)*** or legal advisor would be conclusive

# 9.1 The fully secret trust

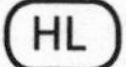

## McCormick v Grogan (1869) LR 4 HL 82

**Key Facts**

A testator left his property to Mr Grogan under a short will. He became very seriously ill and he told Grogan that his will and a letter could be found in his desk. The letter contained the names of certain beneficiaries and gifts that they were to receive, although he added these words: 'I do not wish you to act strictly to the foregoing instructions, but leave it entirely to your own good judgment to do as you think I would if living, and as the parties are deserving.'

**Key Law**

It was held that no trust was created because the testator did not intend to impose a trust on the executor.

## HC Ottaway v Norman [1972] Ch 698

**Key Facts**

Miss Hodges lived with Harry Ottaway in his house and he left it to her in his will. She in turn left it to Mr and Mrs Norman. Harry Ottaway's son claimed that she held the house for him under a secret trust and so she had no right to leave it to others on her death. The judge held that a fully secret trust had been created and so the son had a valid claim.

**Key Law**

A fully secret trust must satisfy three requirements:

(i) intention;
(ii) communication; and
(iii) acceptance.

# 9.1.1 Intention

## CA Re Snowden [1979] Ch 528

**Key Facts**

The testatrix left her estate to her brother. She was not certain how to distribute it amongst her relatives. Some days before her death she announced her brother 'would know what to do'. She died and a few days later the brother died. He had made a will in favour of his son. The question before the court was whether the son could inherit the estate, or whether it was held on secret trust for all the nephews and nieces.

It was held that the words only imposed a moral obligation on him and did not show an intention to create a trust

## 9.1.2 Communication

### (CA) Wallgrave v Tebbs (1855) 2 K & J 313

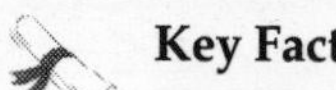

**Key Facts**

Property was left under a will to the defendants absolutely. A letter was found after the testator's death which showed an intention that the defendants should apply the property to a charitable purpose connected with the church. As this intention was not communicated until after the death of the testator, the defendants were entitled to take the property absolutely.

### (HC) Re Stead [1900] 1 Ch 237

**Key Facts**

The testatrix left property to two beneficiaries, Mrs Witham and Mrs Andrews, as tenants in common. She told Mrs Witham that the property was to be held on secret trust for another. The other tenant in common, Mrs Andrews, was not informed. Since the terms of the trusts had not been communicated to the second tenant in common, it was held that her share was free of the trust.

**Key Comment**

The position would be different if the trustees held as joint tenants. If only one was informed of the secret trust then both would be bound.

### (HC) Re Boyes (1884) LR 26 Ch D 531

**Key Facts**

The testator, George Boyes, left his entire estate to his solicitor. He told him he would communicate the terms of the trust by letter. There was no communication whilst the testator was alive, but papers were discovered after his death which made provision for the solicitor to hold the property for the testator's mistress and illegitimate child.

There could be no enforceable secret trust because the terms had not been communicated during the testator's lifetime. The property could not be claimed by the testator because he was aware that it was held for another, so it reverted back to the testator's next of kin.

## Re Cooper [1939] Ch 811

**Key Facts**

A testator left £5,000 by will to two trustees. He had communicated the existence of the trust to them both. Later he added a codicil which increased the amount to £10,000 but he did not communicate the alteration to them both. It was held that only the £5,000 was subject to the trust.

### 9.1.3 Acceptance

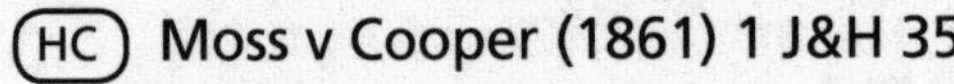

## HC Moss v Cooper (1861) 1 J&H 352

**Key Facts**

Property was left jointly between three trustees. The testator told all three of them the terms of the bequest, which was that they should transfer the property to named charities after his death. Only two of the three trustees accepted the trust, the third did not refuse the trust but remained silent. It was held that silence can constitute acceptance of a trust.

# 9.2 The half-secret trust

## HL Blackwell v Blackwell [1929] AC 318

**Key Facts**

The testator left a legacy to trustees to apply the income 'for the purposes indicated by me to them...'. This was enforced as a half-secret trust.

**Key Law**

In a half-secret trust there must be intention, communication and acceptance of the trust. The communication must be before the will is executed, or at the same time.

**Key Judgment**

**Lord Sumner:** 'A testator cannot reserve himself a power of making future unwitnessed dispositions by merely naming a trustee and leaving the purposes of the trust to be supplied afterwards…'.

## Re Keen [1937] Ch 236

**Key Facts**

The testator gave a sum of money to trustees 'to be held on trust and disposed of by them among such person or persons or charities as may be notified by me to them or either of them during my lifetime.'

He handed a sealed envelope to the trustees which contained the names of the beneficiaries of the intended trust.

**Key Law**

It was held that this could be a valid communication of the terms of the secret trust, but in this case it was inconsistent with the terms of the will.

**Key Judgment**

**Lord Wright MR:** 'To take a parallel, a ship which sails under sealed orders is sailing under orders though the exact terms are not ascribed by the Captain till later.'

## Re Rees W T [1950] Ch 204

**Key Facts**

Trustees of a half-secret trust had been told by the testator that he wished them to make certain payments and to retain the surplus for themselves. It was held that they could not keep the sum for themselves, since the will had imposed a trust over the whole of his estate

# 9.3 Issues arising in secret trusts

## Re Gardner (No 2) [1923] 2 Ch 230

**Key Facts**

A testatrix had left her estate to her husband for life and then to her nieces under a secret trust. One of the nieces predeceased her. It was held that the gift to the niece took effect when the will was executed and her estate could benefit.

**Key Comment**

This decision has been criticised as it undermines the main principle of the secret trust, which is that it is a trust which becomes fully constituted on the death of the testator.

### Re Young [1951] Ch 344

**Key Facts**

A chauffeur had witnessed the will of his employer. He left his entire estate to his wife. He had privately told her to hold a sum for the chauffeur on his death. It was held that this gift should be upheld in spite of s 15 Wills Act 1837, which prevents a witness from benefiting from a will that he/she witnesses.

# 9.4 Mutual wills

## 9.4.1 Agreement to be bound

### HC Re Oldham [1925] Ch 75

**Key Facts**

The parties had made wills in similar form leaving their property to each other absolutely. After the death of the husband the wife married and made a new will on different terms. It was held that the original wills were identical but not intended to take effect as mutual wills because she had always intended to be bound by the terms of the will.

### HC Re Cleaver [1981] 2 All ER 1018

**Key Facts**

Mr and Mrs Cleaver married when they were both in their seventies. They executed identical wills leaving their estates to the survivor absolutely and in default to the three children of the husband's first marriage. On her husband's death the wife executed a new will leaving her estate to only one of the children. It was held that the wife's estate was held on the terms of the mutual wills because she had always intended to be bound by the terms of the will.

## 9.4.2 Consideration

### (HC) Re Dale [1994] Ch 31

**Key Facts**

A husband and wife both agreed to execute wills leaving each other's estate to their son and daughter equally. The husband died first and the wife made a new will leaving her estate to her son with a small gift to her daughter.

**Key Law**

It was held that the estate was held on trust for both the children in equal shares. The consideration in a mutual will was not of benefit to the surviving spouse but was the fact that the first party had executed a mutual will and then had not taken advantage of his right to revoke it in his/her lifetime.

## 9.4.3 Evidence of the mutual will

### (HC) Goodchild v Goodchild [1997] 3 All ER 63

**Key Facts**

The parties had executed similar wills. After the death of the wife the husband had met a new wife and he had executed a new will in her favour. The son, who stood to benefit under the original will, sought to challenge the new will on the basis that the first wills had been mutual wills. He failed to prove that they had been mutual wills, because there was not sufficient evidence that the parties had intended to be bound when they were executed. The solicitor gave evidence that he did not think that the parties had intended the wills to be mutual.

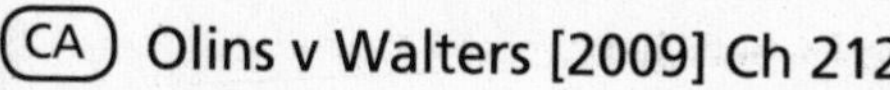

### (CA) Olins v Walters [2009] Ch 212

**Key Facts**

A husband and wife made mutual wills in 1988 and later in 1998 the husband and wife executed similar codicils agreeing not to revoke their existing wills. The wife died in 2006 and the husband argued that he was not bound by the mutual wills. The Court of Appeal found that the husband was bound because there was evidence of a contract between the parties which was binding on the death of the wife and the husband then held the estate as a constructive trustee.

**Key Judgment**
**Mummery LJ**: 'it is a legally necessary condition of mutual wills that there is clear and satisfactory evidence of a contract between two testators'.

# 10

# *Resulting and Constructive Trusts*

## Automatic Resulting Trusts

***Re Ames Settlement (1946)***
Where a valid trust fails for any reason the remaining property will be held on resulting trust for the settlor

***Vandervell v IRC (1967)***
Where a trust fails the surplus assets will be held on resulting trust for the settlor even if the transferor did not intend a trust to arise

***Barclays Bank v Quistclose (1970)***

## Presumed Resulting Trusts

***Dyer v Dyer (1788)***
A trust of a legal estate will result to the man who advances the purchase money

## Constructive Trusts

***Binions v Evans (1972)***
Property will be held on constructive trust where it has been purchased expressly subject to the rights of another and equity will not allow such rights to be denied

**The remedial constructive trust**

***Re Polly Peck (No 5) (1998)***
This is not recognised in the UK

**The institutional constructive trust**
Traditionally recognised by the UK

## Trust fund not fully exhausted

***Re Gillingham Bus Disaster Fund (1958)***
Where unknown contributors had contributed for a named purpose which fails the fund will be held on resulting trust for the contributors

***Re Abbott Fund Trusts (1900)***
Money collected for the care of two elderly inhabitants of a village was held on resulting trust after their death

***Re Osoba (1979)***
A fund left for the education of the settlor's daughter could be claimed absolutely by her after she had completed her university education

## Land

***Hodgson v Marks (1971)***
Where no written declaration of trust has been made to conform with s 53(1)(b) the interest can still be held under an implied trust which does not need to comply with written formalities

***Laskar v Laskar (2008)***

## Personalty

***Re Vinogradoff (1935)***
A minor could hold personalty on resulting trust for another but never land.

## The use of the Constructive Trust

***Lysaght v Edwards (1876)***
The vendor becomes a constructive trustee in a contract for sale of land

***Neville v Wilson (1997)***

***Lyus v Prowsa Developments (1982)***
A constructive trust will arise where a purchaser purchases expressly subject to the rights of a third party

## Constructive Trusts of the family home

***Oxley v Hiscock (2004)***

***Midland Bank v Cooke (1995)***

***Stack v Dowden (2007)***

***Fowler v Barron (2008)***

## The dissolution of an unincorporated association

***Re West Sussex Constabulary's Widows (1971)***
The surviving members had no claim over a fund that had been established for widows of members of the constabulary in West Sussex. The fund went *bona vacantia* to the Crown
***Re Bucks Constabulary Widows and Orphans Fund Friendly Society (No 2) (1979)***
Surplus funds left after the dissolution of a friendly society were held to pass to the members alive at the date of dissolution

## Surplus funds in a pension fund

***Davis v Richards and Wallington Industries Ltd (1991)***
A surplus in a pension fund was held to pass to the Crown after the employers had been able to claim overpayments to the fund
***Air Jamaica v Charlton (1999)***
A pension fund surplus could be claimed by the employers as well as the members

## Presumption of advancement and rebuttal of presumption of resulting trust

***Re Roberts (1946)***
There was a presumption of advancement from father to son
***Bennet v Bennet (1879)***
There was no presumption of advancement from mother to child
***Pettitt v Pettitt (1970)***
Lord Diplock criticised the presumption of advancement between husband and wife in this case, but in spite of attempts to introduce legislation to reform this, the presumption remains

## Rebuttal of a resulting trust

***Fowkes v Pascoe (1875)***
Property purchased in joint names of the transferor and the transferee were not held on resulting trust if evidence suggests they were to be a gift
***Re Sharpe (a Bankrupt) (1980)***
Where there is evidence of a loan there is no presumption of a resulting trust

## Transfers for illegal purposes

***Tinsley v Milligan (1994)***
Where an illegal purpose exists but does not have to be relied on by the claimant it will not affect a finding of a resulting trust
***Tribe v Tribe (1996)***

# 10.1 Definition of automatic and presumed resulting trusts

## Westdeutsche & Landesbank Girozentrale v Islington LBC [1996] (above, Chap 2)

**Key Facts**

Money was lent by Westdeutsche, a German bank, to the Borough of Islington in 'an interest swap agreement' which was later found to be a void agreement. The bank brought a claim for compound interest, rather than simple interest which could only be paid if the money had been held on trust by the local authority.

**Key Law**

The liability of the local authority to repay the loan from Westdeutsche under the *ultra vires* agreement was subject only to a personal liability to repay because the bank had intended the local authority to become absolute owners of the fund. Their liability to repay lay in common law and not in equity, therefore since the claim lay in common law only simple interest could be claimed. Compound interest is only payable under equity.

**Key Judgment**

**Lord Browne-Wilkinson:** 'The local authority had no knowledge of the invalidity of the contract but regarded the money as its own to spend as it thought fit. There was never a time at which both (a) there was defined trust property, and (b) the conscience of the local authority in relation to such defined trust property was affected. The basic requirements of a trust was never satisfied…'

He identified the following two sets of circumstances when a trust will arise:

(1) Where A makes a voluntary payment to B or pays (wholly or in part) for the purchase of property which is vested either to B or pays (wholly or in part) for the purchase of property which is vested either in B alone or in joint names of A and B, there is a presumption that A did not intend to make a gift to B.

(2) Where A transfers property to B on express trusts but the trust declared does not exhaust the whole beneficial interest.

## Re Vandervell's Trusts (No 2) [1974] 1 All ER 47 (see facts of earlier case above)

**Key Facts**

This case concerned the issues arising about ownership of the shares transferred to the Royal College of Pharmacology by Mr Vandervell. It was held that he had retained sufficient interest for the shares to be held on resulting trust for him. Since the court held the shares were held on resulting trust for Mr Vandervell, the transfer of his interest by the trustees to a trust for his children did not require writing. Implied trusts are excluded from the operation of s 53(1)(c).

**Key Law**

Resulting trusts can be classified onto two categories, 'automatic' and 'presumed'. Automatic resulting trusts arise where there is a gap in the ownership, and presumed resulting trusts arise where property is purchased in the name of another and the title is held on presumed resulting trust for the party providing the purchase money.

**Key Link**

Formalities **Chapter 6**.

# 10.2 Automatic resulting trusts

An automatic resulting trust arises '… where A transfers property to B *on express trusts*, but the trusts declared do not exhaust the whole of the beneficial interest.' Lord Browne-Wilkinson in *Westdeutsche Landesbank Girozentrale v Islington London Borough Council* (1996).

## 10.2.1 Failure of an express trust

### Re Ames Settlement [1946] Ch 217

**Key Facts**

A marriage settlement was created by a father in favour of his son. The marriage was later declared void due to the husband's incapacity to consummate the marriage and as a result there was total failure of consideration of the marriage settlement. The property was held to result back to the father's estate.

**Key Law**

If a valid trust is created and then later fails, any property remaining in the fund will be held on resulting trust for the settlor.

HL Barclays Bank v Quistclose (1970)

(see **Chapter 2**)

HC Cooper v PRG Powerhouse Ltd (in Liquidation) [2008] 2 AER 964

**Key Facts**

Mr Cooper was employed by a company and was provided with a car for which he made payments. After he resigned he paid a sum for the outstanding amount for the car but before it could be transferred to the car manufacturers, the company went into liquidation. The employee successfully argued that the money paid was held for a purpose and was therefore held on trust by the company and since the purpose had failed it should be returned to him.

## 10.2.2 Trust fund not fully exhausted

HC Re Gillingham Bus Disaster Fund [1958] Ch 300

**Key Facts**

A number of marine cadets were killed or seriously injured in an accident and a large sum of money was collected for the care of the survivors and also for 'worthy causes'. There was a surplus after the injured had been cared for. The secondary cause was not charitable. The court found the surplus funds were held on resulting trust for the contributors.

**Key Law**

The subscribers had intended to contribute to a specific purpose and that had now failed, so each donor retained an interest, which resulted back to them.

HC Re Abbott Fund Trusts [1900] 2 Ch 326

**Key Facts**

A sum of money was collected in a village for two deaf and dumb old ladies. On their death there was a surplus in the fund.

**Key Law**

The surplus could not be claimed by the next of kin but was held on resulting trust for the subscribers on the basis that the contributors had transferred their fund on express trust for the care of the two old ladies and that purpose had now failed.

## Re Osoba [1979] 1 WLR 247

**Key Facts**

Property was left on trust for the testator's widow, the maintenance and training of his daughter up to university grade, and for the maintenance of his aged mother. Both the widow and the testator's mother had died and the daughter had completed her university education. The court held that the gifts were intended to be absolute and the reference to maintenance and education were words of motive. The daughter was therefore entitled to keep the surplus.

**Key Link**

Compare *Barclays Bank v Quistclose Investments Ltd* (1970), at **5.2.1** above, where a resulting trust arose when the primary trust had failed.

# 10.2.3 The dissolution of an unincorporated association

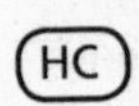

## Re West Sussex Constabulary's Widows, Children and Benevolent (1930) Fund Trusts [1971] Ch 1

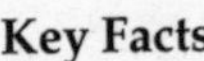

**Key Facts**

A fund was established to provide benefits for widows and dependants of members of the West Sussex Constabulary. The money was collected from a number of sources including raffles, subscriptions, entertainments, sweepstakes and collecting boxes as well as legacies. The West Sussex Constabulary was combined with other police forces, leaving a surplus in this fund.

**Key Law**

It was held that the surviving members had no claim at all because they had received all that they had contracted for and the money was paid on the basis of contract and not of trust. A similar view was taken over the raffles, subscriptions, entertainments and sweepstakes. The funds from outside legacies were held on resulting trust for the subscribers and the remainder went *bona vacantia* to the Crown.

## Re Bucks Constabulary Widows and Orphans Fund Friendly Society (No 2) [1979] 1 WLR 936

**Key Facts**

A fund was set up to provide benefits for the widows and orphans of deceased police officers and the provision of payments on the death of a member or during sickness. When the Bucks Constabulary wound up there was a surplus in the fund. The court held that the fund would be held for the members alive at the date of dissolution and would be split between them.

**Key Law**

This is a contractual solution to the problem of surplus funds in an unincorporated association. Walton J suggested that there would be only one circumstance when the property would be held *bona vacantia* to the Crown, and that would be where the association was reduced to only one member.

**Key Problem**

There are inherent problems with surplus funds on the dissolution of an unincorporated association. There are a number of solutions: there could be a resulting trust for those who had contributed for a purpose, there could be distribution between the members of the association, or the money could pass *bona vacantia* to the Crown. It could be argued that where it is held *bona vacantia* for the Crown, the Crown has made an unexpected gain in the circumstances and the members always have a stronger claim to any surplus funds.

### 10.2.4 Surplus funds in a pension fund

HC Davis v Richards and Wallington Industries Ltd [1991] 2 All ER 563

**Key Facts**

A surplus remained in a pension fund after the pensioners' claims had been met. It was held that it could pass under resulting trust to the contributors unless expressly excluded. Rules excluded the employees from claiming a share but the employers had a right to claim a share in proportion to their overpayments. The remaining surplus passed *bona vacantia* to the Crown.

PC Air Jamaica v Charlton [1999] 1 WLR 1399

**Key Facts**

A pension fund surplus arose and the court, following *Davis v Richards*, held that the surplus could be held on resulting trust but in this case it would be for both the employers as well as the members. The shares would be calculated *pro rata* between surviving members and the dependants of deceased members in proportion to their contributions.

## 10.3 Presumed resulting trusts

HC Dyer v Dyer (1788) 2 Cox Eq Cas 92

**Key Judgment**

**Eyre CB:** 'The trust of a legal estate, whether taken in the names of the purchasers and others jointly or in the names of others without that of the purchaser; whether in one name or several; whether jointly or successive — results to the man who advances the purchase money.'

## 10.3.1 Land

### CA Hodgson v Marks [1971] Ch 892

**Key Facts**

Mrs Hodgson transferred her house to her lodger on the oral understanding that she would be able to remain there and that he would look after her affairs. There was no written agreement complying with s 53(1)(b) LPA 1925 which holds that an express trust of land must be made in writing in order to be enforceable. The lodger sold the house to a *bona fide* purchaser, Mr Marks.

**Key Law**

The court held that Mrs Hodgson retained an interest in the property as the lodger had held the property on resulting trust after the transfer to him, and Mrs Hodgson's interest remained binding on the purchaser.

**Key Comment**

Recently it appears that courts no longer regard resulting trusts as an appropriate way of discovering common intention between the parties in the context of land. (see *Stack v Dowden* **below**). However, Lord Neuberger in a dissenting judgment in *Stack v Dowden* suggested that the resulting trust may still be useful in this context. The appropriate situation identified in recent cases is where property is purchased as an investment. Even between family members this will be regarded as held under a resulting trust.

**Key Link**

Note that the formalities for the creation of a trust in land had not been complied with but under s 53(2) a resulting trust does not require any formalities.

### CA Laskar v Laskar [2008] EWCA 347

**Key Facts**

A mother and daughter purchased property primarily as an investment property and not to be a home they could enjoy jointly. The court applied a resulting trust when deciding on their shares in the property.

### 10.3.2 Personalty

HC Re Vinogradoff [1935] WN 68

**Key Facts**

A grandmother transferred by way of gift £800 worth of war loan stock into the joint names of herself and her granddaughter, who was aged four. The grandmother continued to receive the dividends. Under her will the stock passed to another and it was held that the granddaughter held it on resulting trust for the grandmother's estate.

## 10.4 Presumption of advancement and rebuttal of presumption of resulting trusts

### 10.4.1 Father to child

HC Re Roberts [1946] Ch 1

**Key Facts**

A father took out an insurance policy on the life of his son and paid premiums on it. After the father's death a claim was made on behalf of the estate that the premiums were recoverable from the policy. This was rejected, although subsequent premiums paid after his death would be recoverable.

**Key Law**

Each of the premiums was seen as a separate advancement to his son.

### 10.4.2 Mother to child

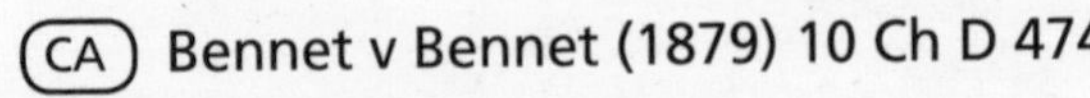

CA Bennet v Bennet (1879) 10 Ch D 474

**Key Judgment**

**Jessel MR:** 'We arrive then at this conclusion, that in the case of a mother … it is easier to prove a gift than in the case of a stranger; in the case of a mother very little evidence beyond the relationship is wanted, there being very little additional motive required to induce a mother to make a gift to her child …'.

## 10.4.3 Husband to wife

### HL Pettitt v Pettitt [1970] AC 777

**Key Facts**

A husband made contributions in kind towards the matrimonial home, which was registered in the name of his wife. The court held that the wife did not hold the property on resulting trust for him and he had no share in the property based on his contributions in kind.

**Key Judgment**

**Lord Diplock:** 'It would … be an abuse of the legal technique for ascertaining or imputing intention to apply to transactions between the post-war generation of married couples "presumptions" which are based upon inferences of fact which an earlier generation of judges drew as the most likely intentions of earlier generations of spouses belonging to the propertied classes of a different social era …'.

**Key Comment**

Although the presumption of advancement between husband and wife has been subject to criticism it remains and attempts to abolish it have failed.

### HC Abrahams v Trustee in Bankruptcy of Abrahams [1999] BPIR 637

**Key Facts**

A wife contributed to a syndicate for the purchase of lottery tickets in the name of herself and her husband. The syndicate won and it was held that the presumption of advancement did not operate in favour of the husband. As a result, the wife could claim both shares because the husband held his share of the winnings on resulting trust for his wife.

## 10.4.4 Rebuttal of the presumption of a resulting trust

### (CA) Fowkes v Pascoe (1875) 10 Ch App 343

**Key Facts**

Annuities were purchased by Sarah Baker in the joint names of herself and John Pascoe, raising a presumption of a resulting trust. This was rebutted by evidence that a gift was intended. She had purchased some of the stock in her sole name and some in joint names of herself and another.

**Key Law**

The court found that as she held the shares in separate shareholdings, this was evidence that a gift was intended.

### (HC) Re Sharpe (a Bankrupt) [1980] 1 WLR 219

**Key Facts**

Property had been purchased by a nephew with a contribution of his aunt. When he became bankrupt she claimed a share in the property under a resulting trust. It was held that the contribution was a loan and no resulting trust arose. However, the court did not find in favour of the aunt on the basis of proprietary estoppel.

## 10.4.5 Transfers for illegal purposes

### (HL) Tinsley v Milligan [1994] 1 AC 340

**Key Comment**

The claimant relied on a presumption of a resulting trust and did not need to base her claim on the illegal purpose, so the court was able to find in favour of the claimant.

→ **Key Link**

See **1.1 The development of equity**.

### (CA) Tribe v Tribe [1996] Ch 107

**Key Facts**

A father transferred shares into the name of his son with the express purpose of minimising his assets to prevent his landlord from recovering a contribution towards essential repairs on the property which he rented. The repairs were carried out without the father having to pay for them, so he tried to recover the shares from his son who refused to return them. The court held that they must be returned in spite of the illegal motive. Although the presumption of advancement may have applied, the father could rely on the presumption of a resulting trust. Although the reasons for the transfer were illegal, i.e. to defraud the creditors, the illegal purpose had not been carried out.

**Key Comment**

In 2009 the Law Commission recommended that the law on illegality should be replaced with a statutory discretion for the court to declare the trust to be illegal or invalid. This would have allowed the House of Lords to declare the trust in *Tinsley v Milligan* invalid as it would not depend on whether or not the parties had relied on the illegality. However the Law Commission has recommended that the illegality should only have an effect on the beneficial entitlement where there are exceptional circumstances.

## 10.5 Definition of a constructive trust

### Binions v Evans [1972] Ch 359

**Key Facts**

A widow was given a contractual licence by her deceased husband's employers to remain in a house for the rest of her life. Later she was served with an eviction notice by third party purchasers. It was held that they held the house on constructive trust for her because they bought expressly subject to her rights and bought at undervalue.

**Key Judgment**

**Lord Denning MR:** 'A constructive trust is the formula through which the conscience of equity finds expression. When property has been acquired in such circumstances that the holder of the legal title may not in good conscience retain the beneficial interest, equity converts him into a trustee.'

## 10.6 Categories of constructive trust

### 10.6.1 The remedial constructive trust

(CA) Polly Peck (No 5) [1998] 3 All ER 812

**Key Facts**

The claimants owned land in Cyprus and they claimed the right to proceed against the administrators of Polly Peck International. They claimed that they were entitled to a share of the profits that Polly Peck had made by exploiting their land after it had been misappropriated by the Turkish republic of Northern Cyprus. They based their claim on a remedial constructive trust. This would allow them to gain priority over the creditors.

The claim was rejected and it was commented by Nourse LJ in the case that the remedial constructive trust could only be introduced into English law by Act of Parliament.

**Key Comment**

English law traditionally only recognises the institutional constructive trust. This is brought into being on the occurrence of specified events without the need for the intervention of the courts.

## 10.7 The use of the constructive trust

### 10.7.1 Specifically enforceable contract to sell property

(HC) Lysaght v Edwards (1876) 2 Ch D 499

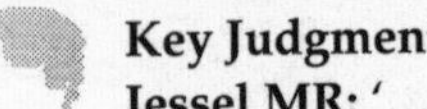

**Key Judgment**

**Jessel MR:** '… the moment you have a valid contract for sale the vendor becomes a trustee in equity for the purchaser of the estate sold, and the beneficial ownership passes to the purchaser …'.

### 10.7.2 Sale of shares in a private company

Neville v Wilson [1997] (above, Chap 6)

**Key Law**

Where specific performance of a contract would have been available, a constructive trust will arise. In this case there was a contract to purchase shares in a private company which is specifically enforceable.

### 10.7.3 Where a purchaser takes expressly subject to third party rights

HC Lyus v Prowsa Developments [1982] 1 WLR 1044

**Key Facts**

Mr and Mrs Lyus had entered into a contract to purchase a house to be built on a new estate. The developers went into liquidation and the bank sold the house to another developer, expressly subject to the rights of Mr and Mrs Lyus.

When the land was sold to others it was held that the couple had rights under a constructive trust which were binding on the purchasers.

## 10.8 Constructive trusts in land

### 10.8.1 Where the legal title of the land is in a sole name

Lloyds Bank v Rosset [1991] 1 AC 107

**Key Facts**

A married couple purchased a house. It was registered in the husband's sole name and he provided the purchase money. The wife contributed towards the renovation of the property and claimed a share in equity. It was held that she did not have a share because she could not prove that there was a common intention to share the property.

**Key Law**

A common intention to share must either be expressly agreed in which case contributions in kind can be evidence of detriment, or it can be inferred in which case only contributions to the purchase money will be sufficient evidence of intention.

Where one party claims a share in property based on rights in equity there must be proof of a common intention to share the property. A common intention to share can either be express or implied but in each case there must be evidence of detriment. Where the common intention is expressly agreed then contributions in kind will qualify as detriment. In cases of implied common intention only financial contributions towards the purchase price will be sufficient evidence of common intention.

**Key Problem**

Common intention can often be difficult to prove because people do not always discuss shares in property but make assumptions about ownership.

## (CA) Grant v Edwards [1986] Ch 638

**Key Facts**

A couple set up home together. The woman was married to another man. A house was purchased and registered in the sole name of the man, because he thought it would prejudice her entitlement on divorce if the house was registered in joint names. The court held that this was sufficient evidence of a common intention to share ownership.

**Key Link**

*Eves v Eves* [1975] 1 WLR 1328

## Eves v Eves [1975] 1 WLR 1328

**Key Facts**

An unmarried couple moved in together in property owned by Mr Eves. He told the woman that he had intended to put her name on the title but he thought (wrongly) that she was too young because she was only 18. The court held that there was sufficient proof of an intention to share the title and she was awarded a quarter share.

## 10.8.2 Quantification of the shares under a constructive trust

### CA Midland Bank plc v Cooke [1995] 4 AER 562

**Key Facts**

A common intention to share was found here because the wife had made a financial contribution (albeit very small) to the purchase of the property. When quantifying the shares the court held that it was entitled to look at 'the whole course of dealing' between the parties and as it was clear the parties shared both income and expenditure equally the beneficial interest in the property was split equally between them.

### CA Oxley v Hiscock [2005] Fam 211

**Key Facts**

Where shares under a constructive trust are being quantified and the courts cannot identify an assumed intention between the parties as to how the shares are to be divided, the courts have a broad discretion to award what share they feel is 'fair' in all the circumstances. This principle was disapproved of in the case of *Stack v Dowden*.

## 10.8.3 Where legal title is in joint names

### HL Stack v Dowden [2007] 2 AC 432

**Key Facts**

This case concerned quantifying shares in a family home jointly owned by an unmarried couple with four children and who had been together for 25 years. The first house of the couple had been purchased and funded by Ms Dowden. However the property in question was partly funded by Mr Stack who contributed 35 per cent whilst Ms Dowden contributed the rest.

The House of Lords disapproving of the 'fairness' principle from *Oxley v Hiscock* held that the general rule should be that 'equity should follow the law' so in most cases where the legal title is jointly owned the beneficial interests should be split equally unless there were exceptional circumstances. In this case circumstances were exceptional because the parties had kept their finances separate throughout their relationship and the equitable interest was shared 65 per cent/35 per cent.

**Key Judgment**

**Lady Hale:** '... cases in which the joint legal owners are to be taken to have intended that their beneficial interest should be different from their legal interests will be very unusual ... .'

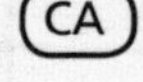

## CA Fowler v Barron [2008] EWCA Civ 377

**Key Facts**

The family home was owned jointly by this couple but whereas Mr Barron paid all the expense on the property, Ms Fowler paid ancillary expenses such as clothes for the family. However, there was nothing to rebut the presumption that equity follows the law.

# 11

# *Charitable Trusts*

***IRC v Pemsel (1891)***
Lord Macnaghten held that there were four charitable purposes: trusts for the relief of poverty; trusts for the advancement of education; trusts for the advancement of religion and trusts for other purposes beneficial to the community. The meaning of a charitable purpose has now been defined in legislation but includes the main purposes listed in *Pemsel's Case*.

## The Charities Act 2006

A charitable gift must fall within the categories in the Charities Act 2006. These include the advancement of education; religion; health or saving of lives; citizenship or community development; arts, culture, heritage or science; amateur sport; human rights, conflict resolution; environmental protection; the relief of those in need by reason of youth, age, ill-health, disability; the advancement of animal welfare; the promotion of the efficiency of the armed forces; and any other purpose

## Trusts for the relief of poverty

This can cover a wide variety of circumstances
***Re Scarisbrick (1951)***
Needy relatives
***Re Segelman (1996)***
Relatives who were poor and needy
***Re Coulthurst (1951)***
Poverty can mean 'to go short' in the ordinary acceptance of the term
***Re Sanders Will Trusts (1954)***
No charitable trust to assist the working classes as working classes need not be poor

## Trusts for the advancement of education

***Re Besterman Wills Trusts (1980)***
An educational trust will be charitable if it is a useful subject for research, the subject matter is disseminated to others and it is for the benefit of the public or a sufficient section of it
***Royal Choral Society v IRC (1943)***
***Re Shaw (1958)***
A trust for research into a 40-letter alphabet failed
***Re Pinion (1965)***
A fund of artefacts was not charitable because the court held it lacked any artistic merit
***IRC v McMullen (1981)***
A trust to promote sport or to provide sports facilities will not be upheld unless it is associated with education

## Trusts for the advancement of religion

***Bowman v Secular Society (1917)***
Only monotheistic faiths could qualify as a religion
***Re South Place Ethical Society (1980)***
Religion did not include ethical purposes
***Re Watson (1973)***
A religion with very few followers with little merit in their beliefs could still qualify as a religion

## Trusts for any other purpose beneficial to the community

***Williams v IRC (1947)***
Traditionally these charitable purposes would only be charitable if they came within the preamble to the Charitable Uses Act 1601
**Animals**
***Re Wedgwood (1915)***
The protection and benefit of animals is charitable because it encourages people to be humane and generous.
***Re Grove-Grady (1929)***
No public benefit because the public were unable to view the animal refuge.
**Sporting and recreational charities**
***Re Nottage (1895)***
Sport is not charitable *per se*
***IRC v City of Glasgow Police Athletic Association (1953)***
***Guild v IRC (1992)***
A sports centre can be charitable under the Recreational Charities Act 1958
**Relief of the sick**
***Re Resch's Will Trust (1969)***
Funds left to a private hospital could be for charitable purposes

## The new categories of charitable purposes under the Charities Act

These include:

The advancement of health;

The advancement of citizenship;

The advancement of the arts;

The advancement of amateur sport;

Advancement of human rights;

Advancement of animal welfare;

Promotion of the effeciency of the armed forces.

## The public benefit test

**s 3 Charities Act 2006**
A charitable purpose under the Act must be for the public benefit
A charitable purpose is not presumed to be for the public benefit. It must be demonstrated that it is for the public benefit
Public benefit means an identifiable benefit, it must be clear and related to the aims of the charity and balanced against any detriment or harm. If only a section of the public is to benefit there must be no geographical or financial restrictions. Private benefits must be incidental and people in poverty must not be excluded

## The restrictions placed must not be arbitrary

***IRC v Baddeley (1955)***
A charity will not satisfy the public benefit test if it benefits a 'class within a class'

## Non-charitable benefits must be incidental

A trust can still be regarded as charitable where the main purpose of the body is charitable but it contains some non-charitable purposes
***IRC v City of Glasgow Athletic Association (1953)***
***Re Coxen (1948)***
***Funnell v Stewart (1996)***

## The personal nexus rule

Traditionally a trust has not been upheld as charitable if the class to benefit are dependent on a personal nexus with the settlor
***Oppenheim v Tobacco Securities Trust Co Ltd (1951)***
***Dingle v Turner (1972)***
There were some anomalous exceptions pre-2006
***Re Scarisbrick (1951)*** (poor relations)
***Re Segelman (1995)***

## Cy-pres

A charitable trust for a purpose that has failed may succeed on the principle of cy-près allowing the funds to be transferred to another similar charity if there is evidence of a general charitable intent
***Re Faraker (1912)***
There will be no failure of the charity if the charity has not ceased to exist but been amalgamated with another charity
***Re Spence (1979)***
***Re Rymer (1895)***
There is no evidence of general charitable intent where the gift is very specific in nature
***Biscoe v Jackson (1887)***
General charitable intent shown
***Re Harwood (1936)***
A gift for a society which has never existed can show charitable intent
***Re Finger's Will Trusts (1972)***
A trust for an unincorporated charity which ceases to exist can be upheld as a trust for purposes but a gift to an incorporated charity which ceases to exist will fail

## Political purposes

***McGovern v Att-Gen (1982)***
A trust cannot be charitable if its main purpose is to secure a change in the law
***Re Hopkinson (1949)***
If the trust appears to be under another purpose but it is really political in nature then it will fail as a charitable trust
***Re Koeppler's Wills Trust (1986)***
A trust to promote greater co-operation in Europe was not political

# 11.1 Definition of charity

## IRC v Pemsel [1891] AC 531

**Key Facts**

Charitable purposes can only be upheld if they fall within four categories: trusts for the relief of poverty; trusts for the advancement of education; trusts for the advancement of religion; and trusts for other purposes beneficial to the community.

**Key Comment**

Traditionally there was no statutory definition of charitable purposes. Before the enactment of the Charities Act 2006 the definition of a charity was largely derived from the preamble of the Statute of Charitable Uses 1601 and the common law in particular *IRC v Pemsel*. The Charities Act 2006 s 2(2) defines and lists charitable purposes:

(a) the prevention of poverty; (b) the advancement of education; (c) the advancement of religion; (d) the advancement of health or the saving of lives; (e) the advancement of citizenship or community development; (f) the advancement of the arts, culture, heritage or science; (g) the advancement of amateur sport; (h) the advancement of human rights, conflict resolution or reconciliation or the promotion of religious or racial harmony or equality and diversity; (i) the advancement of environmental protection or improvement; (j) the relief of those in need by reason of youth, age, ill-health, disability, financial hardship or other disadvantage; (k) the advancement of animal welfare; (i) the promotion of the efficiency of the armed forces of the Crown, or the efficiency of the police, fire and rescue or ambulance services; (m) any other purposes … [recognised by existing charity law].

Previously charitable purposes under the first three heads of charity under *IRC v Pemsel* were presumed to be charitable.

## 11.2 Relief of poverty

Poverty is not defined in the Charities Act. It has traditionally been regarded as a relative concept.

### (CA) Re Scarisbrick [1951] Ch 622

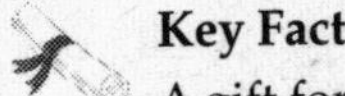

**Key Facts**

A gift for such relations of my son and daughter who 'shall be in needy circumstances' was upheld.

**Key Judgment**

**Jenkins LJ:** '"Poverty" is necessarily to some extent a relative matter, a matter of opinion.'

### (HC) Re Segelman dec'd [1996] 2 WLR 173

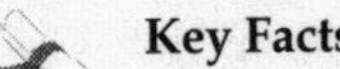

**Key Facts**

A gift to relatives of the testator who were 'poor and needy' was upheld. The class of relatives numbered about 20 people.

### (CA) Re Coulthurst [1951] Ch 661

**Key Facts**

The testator transferred a fund of £20,000 to be paid to widows and orphans of officers of Coutts & Co who the trustees decided were 'the most deserving of such assistance having regard to their financial circumstances'. This was held to be a charitable bequest.

**Key Judgment**

**Lord Evershed MR:** 'It is quite clearly established that poverty does not mean destitution: it is a word of wide and somewhat indefinite import; … meaning persons who have to "go short" in the ordinary acceptance of that term, due regard being had to their status in life.'

### (HC) Re Sanders Will Trusts [1954] Ch 265

**Key Facts**

A testator transferred one-third of his residuary estate 'to provide or assist in providing dwellings for the working classes and their families resident in the area of Pembroke Dock'.

**Key Law**

This was not a charitable gift as the expression 'working classes' was not necessarily a gift to alleviate poverty.

## 11.3 Advancement of education

Traditionally education has been given a broad meaning and is not confined to teaching in schools.

### 11.3.1 Research as education

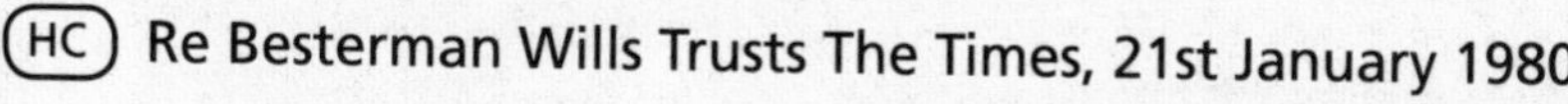

HC Re Besterman Wills Trusts The Times, 21st January 1980

**Key Facts**

A fund to research the works of Voltaire and Rousseau was upheld as charitable because the research met certain criteria.

**Key Law**

A trust for research will only be charitable if:

1. the subject matter of the research is a useful subject of study;
2. the knowledge acquired by the research must be disseminated to others;
3. the trust must be for the benefit of the public, or a sufficiently important section of the public.

HC Re Shaw [1958] 1 All ER 245

**Key Facts**

A gift of money left by George Bernard Shaw for research into a 40-letter alphabet and for the translation of one of his plays into the new alphabet was not charitable.

**Key Problem**

Compare *Re Shaw* and *Re Besterman Wills Trusts*. It is difficult to see the distinction and it is doubtful whether a court today would refuse charitable status to the research proposed in *Re Shaw*.

# 11.3.2 Trusts for the promotion of culture as education

## CA Re Pinion [1965] 1 Ch 85

**Key Facts**

A testator left his studio and the contents to be maintained as a collection to the National Trust. They refused to accept it, although they were willing to accept some items for display. It was held that the collection was not charitable because it lacked any artistic merit.

**Key Comment**

Such a trust today would be considered under the separate head of 'the advancement of the arts'.

**Key Judgment**

**Harman LJ:** 'I can conceive of no useful purpose to be served in foisting upon the public this mass of junk. It has neither public utility nor educative value…'.

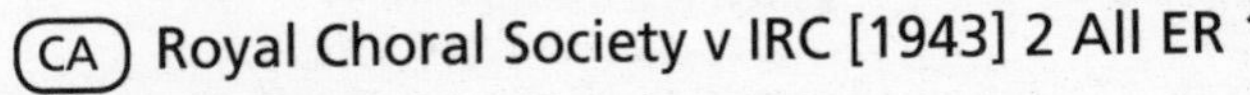

## CA Royal Choral Society v IRC [1943] 2 All ER 101

**Key Facts**

A trust to promote the practice and performance of choral works was upheld as charitable.

**Key Judgment**

**Lord Greene:** 'I protest against that narrow conception of education when one is dealing with aesthetic education. In my opinion, a body of persons established for the purpose of raising the artistic state of the country … is established for educational purposes.'

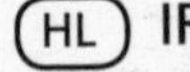

## HL IRC v McMullen [1981] AC 1

**Key Facts**

A trust to provide facilities for pupils at schools and universities in the United Kingdom to play association football or other games or sports was held to be valid by the House of Lords. It was upheld because it was connected with education.

**Key Comment**

Lord Hailsham said in this case that the playing of sport was not charitable *per se*, nor necessarily educational. However, the Charities Act includes the advancement of amateur sport as a separate head of charity.

# 11.4 Advancement of religion

## 11.4.1 What is religion?

Under s 2(3) of the Charities Act, religion includes a religion which involves belief in more than one god, and a religion which does not involve belief in a god. This represents a change in the law.

### Bowman v Secular Society [1917] AC 406

**Key Facts**

It was held by Lord Parker that only monotheistic faiths could qualify as a religion.

**Key Comment**

Lord Parker's very restricted view of what constitutes religion would not be acceptable today under the Charities Act 2006.

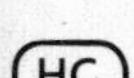

### Re South Place Ethical Society [1980] 1 WLR 1565

**Key Facts**

The society had as one of its aims the 'study and dissemination of ethical principles and the cultivation of a rational religious sentiment'. This was held not to be a charitable purpose because it did not advance religion.

**Key Judgment**

**Dillon J:** 'Religion as I see it, is concerned with man's relations with God, and ethics are concerned with man's relations with man. The two are not the same…'.

### HC Sacred Hands Spiritual Centre's Application for Registration as a Charity [2006] WTLR 873

**Key Facts**

The Charity Commission registered an organisation as a charity which was involved with spiritual healing because it regarded a belief in spiritualists in the spirit world could itself be seen as a faith.

### HC Re Watson [1973] 1 WLR 1472

**Key Facts**

A trust to promote the works of Hobbs, who with the testator was the leading member of a very small group of undenominational Christians, was upheld in spite of the fact that experts regarded the value of their work as nil.

## 11.4.2 Public benefit in religion

### HL Gilmour v Coats [1949] AC 426

**Key Facts**

A gift was left to a Carmelite priory. It consisted of about 20 nuns who lived a cloistered life of prayer and contemplation. They did not involve themselves in work in the community.

**Key Law**

This failed as a charitable trust because it lacked the necessary public benefit. It was held that the value of prayer was not susceptible to proof in a court of law.

### HC Re Hetherington (Dec'd) [1990] Ch 1

**Key Facts**

A gift of money, left for the purpose of saying masses for the dead, was upheld as a valid gift because the masses were said in public and would therefore satisfy the public benefit test.

# 11.5 The new categories of charitable purposes under the Charities Act

## 11.5.1 The advancement of health or saving lives

**Key Law**

Although this appears to be a new category, the purposes have been recognised as charitable before and reflects the preamble to the Statute of Charitable Uses which said 'the relief of the aged, impotent and the poor.'

CA

### Re Smith's Will Trusts [1962] 2 All ER 563

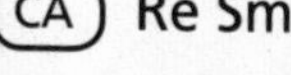

**Key Facts**

A gift of property to be given to such hospitals that the trustees thought fit was held to be charitable.

HC

### London Hospital Medical College v IRC [1976] 1 WLR 613

**Key Law**

A student union at a medical school was granted charitable status on the grounds that it promoted the efficient running of the medical school.

PC

### Re Resch's Will Trusts [1969] 1 AC 514

**Key Law**

A private hospital was held to be charitable although the patients were fee paying because of the benefit provided to the community resulting from the beds and medical staff, nursing etc. which was held to supplement the care provided by the general hospital.

## 11.5.2 The advancement of the arts

**Key Law**

Although trusts which promote art and culture have been recognised for many years, under the advancement of education, the Charities Act now recognises this as a separate heading.

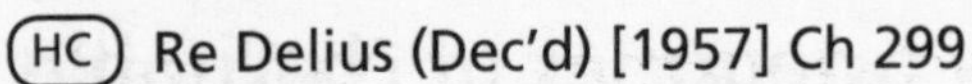

## (HC) Re Delius (Dec'd) [1957] Ch 299

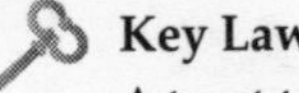

**Key Law**

A trust to promote the music of the composer Frederick Delius was upheld.

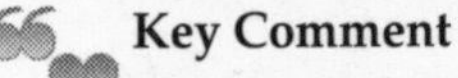

**Key Comment**

To uphold the works of a composer or an artist or a sculptor depends on a value judgment on the artistic merit of a work. In some cases, e.g. a composer such as Delius there would be no challenge but it would be open to any court to seek expert evidence about the artistic merit in any work.

## (CA) Re Pinion (Dec'd) [1965] (see 11.3.2)

## (CA) Royal Choral Society v IRC [1943] (see 11.3.2)

# 11.5.3 The advancement of amateur sport

**Key Law**

It was originally thought that a trust encouraging the playing of sport would not be considered charitable but sport is now included as a separate charitable purpose under the Charities Act.

## (CA) Re Nottage [1895] 2 Ch 649

**Key Facts**

A gift of a prize for yacht-racing was held not to be charitable because the promotion of sport cannot be charitable unless it was for the advancement of education.

## (HL) IRC v McMullen [1981] AC 1 (see **11.3.2**)

## (HL) IRC v City of Glasgow Police Athletic Association [1953] AC 380

**Key Facts**

An association whose object was 'to encourage and promote all forms of athletic sport and general pastimes' was held not to be charitable. It was held that the promotion of the efficiency of the police force would have been charitable but that was held to be incidental to the provision of recreation which was not a charitable purpose and so it failed to gain charitable status.

## 11.5.4 The advancement of animal welfare

### (CA) Re Wedgwood [1915] 1 Ch 113

**Key Facts**

Property was left on trust for the protection and benefit of animals. This was held to be charitable because of the beneficial effect it would have on people, stimulating humane and generous sentiments and promoting feelings of humanity and morality generally.

### (CA) Re Grove-Grady [1929] 1 Ch 557

**Key Facts**

A gift to an animal refuge where animal life of all kinds might be completely undisturbed by man was held not to be charitable, because the public derived no benefit from such a refuge.

**Key Comment**

This case was decided in 1929 and might be treated differently today.

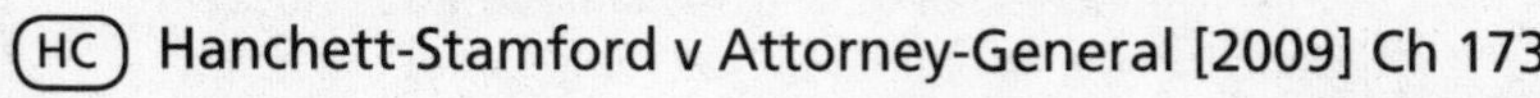

### (HC) Hanchett-Stamford v Attorney-General [2009] Ch 173

**Key Facts**

The Performing and Captive Animals Defence League was refused charitable status in spite of the fact that its purpose was to promote the welfare of animals on the grounds that in order to achieve its purposes it would require a change in the law.

# 11.6 Political trusts

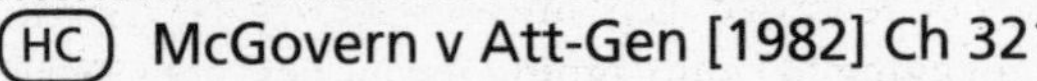

## HC McGovern v Att-Gen [1982] Ch 321

**Key Facts**

Amnesty International wanted to set up a charitable trust for part of its activities. There were four main aspects of its work:

1. Relief of needy persons who were prisoners of conscience and their dependents;
2. Attempting to secure the release of prisoners of conscience;
3. Abolition of torture or inhuman or degrading treatment or punishment;
4. Research into human rights and disseminating the results of research.

Although the first and last purposes were charitable, the others were political in nature and the trust was not charitable.

**Key Law**

A trust cannot be charitable if its main purpose is to secure a change in the law of the United Kingdom or of foreign countries.

## HC Re Hopkinson [1949] 1 All ER 346

**Key Facts**

A gift was made for the advancement of adult education on the lines of a Labour Party memorandum. It was held that this was 'political propaganda masquerading as education'.

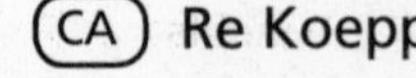

## CA Re Koeppler's Wills Trust [1986] Ch 423

**Key Facts**

A gift of money to Wilton Park was upheld as charitable because it promoted greater co-operation in Europe and was not allied to any political party.

**Key Comment**

The Charity Commission now takes a slightly more relaxed approach to what may be regarded as political purposes, holding that if a charity is not engaging in campaigning or political activity as its sole purpose but merely in order to support its charitable purposes it can carry out some political activity.

## 11.7 Public benefit

### 11.7.1 What constitutes public benefit?

s 3 Charities Act 2006

**Key Law**

A charitable purpose under the Act must be demonstrated that it is for the public benefit. The benefit must be to the public as a whole or a section of the public.

Public benefit is defined as having the same meaning as under previous law, i.e. there must be an identifiable benefit which must be clear and related to the aims of the charity and must be balanced against any detriment or harm. Where the benefit is restricted to a section for the public there must be no geographical or financial restrictions. Private benefits must be incidental and people in poverty must not be excluded from benefitting.

### 11.7.2 The restrictions placed must not be arbitrary

IRC v Baddeley [1955] AC 572

**Key Facts**

A charity will not satisfy the public benefit test if it benefits a 'class within a class'. A gift to the Methodist mission in London for the promotion of the religious, social and physical training of persons resident in West Ham and Leyton 'who were or were likely to become members of the Methodist Church' was held non-charitable. This was because there was a recreational purpose, but the court also decided that the public benefit test was not satisfied because the beneficiaries did not constitute a section of the public.

## 11.7.3 Non-charitable benefits must be incidental

A trust can still be regarded as charitable where the main purpose of the body is charitable but it contains some incidental non-charitable purposes

HL IRC v City of Glasgow Athletic Association (1953) (see 11.5.3)

HC Re Coxen [1948] Ch 747

**Key Facts**

A gift for the benefit of certain hospitals included a sum for a dinner for the trustees and a sum for payment of their expenses. The dinner and payment of expenses were found to be charitable because they promoted better administration of the charity.

HC Funnell v Stewart (1996)

**Key Facts**

A sum of money left in trust for a faith-healing group which held private religious services but saw the faith healing of the community as the main purpose of their work was held to be charitable.

## 11.7.4 The personal nexus rule

**Key Law**

Traditionally a trust has not been upheld as charitable if the class to benefit are dependent on a personal nexus with the settlor.

## Oppenheim v Tobacco Securites Trust Co Ltd [1951] AC 297

**Key Facts**

A testator left a sum of money on his death to be held on trust and the income to be applied for the education of the children of the employees of British American Tobacco. The trust failed because it did not satisfy the public benefit test.

**Key Law**

In order for a trust for education to succeed as a charitable trust the beneficiaries must not be numerically negligible and must not be defined by means of a personal nexus to the settlor.

**Key Judgment**

**Lord Simmonds:** '… a group may be numerous but, if the nexus between them is their personal relationship to a single propositus or to several propositi, they are neither the community nor a section of the community for charitable purposes.'

**Lord Macdermott (dissenting judgment):** 'But can any really fundamental distinction, as respects the personal or impersonal nature of the common link, be drawn between those employed, for example by a particular university and those whom the same university has put in a certain category as the result of individual examination and assessment? Again if the bond between those employed by a particular railway is purely personal, why should the bond between those who are employed as railwaymen be so essentially different?'

## Dingle v Turner [1972] AC 601

**Key Facts**

The testator left his estate to trustees directing them to use the income to provide pensions for poor employees of a company which he jointly owned. It was held to be a valid charitable trust because the personal nexus test does not apply to the relief of poverty.

There were some anomalous exceptions pre-2006.

### (CA) Re Scarisbrick's Will Trusts [1951] Ch 622

**Key Facts**

A testatrix left her residuary estate on trust for her relations 'in needy circumstances' in spite of the personal nexus this was upheld as charitable.

### (HC) Re Segelman (Dec'd) [1996] 2 WLR 173

**Key Facts**

The public benefit test for a trust for the relief of poverty was satisfied where there was a personal nexus between the testator and the beneficiaries.

**Key Comment**

Compare *Oppenheim v Tobacco Securities Trust Co Ltd* [1951] and *Dingle v Turner* [1972] above.

# 11.8 The *cy-près* doctrine

## 11.8.1 No failure of the charity

### (CA) Re Faraker [1912] 2 Ch 488

**Key Facts**

A testatrix left money to Hannah Bayly's Charity. The charity had been founded for poor widows of Rotherhithe but had ceased to exist as a separate charity when it amalgamated with other charities in 1905. The court held that it had not failed but continued in another form, and the funds could be transferred to the amalgamated charities.

## 11.8.2 Evidence of general charitable intent

### (HC) Re Spence [1979] Ch 483

**Key Facts**

Funds were left to 'The Old Folks Home at Hillworth Lodge Keighley', but it had closed down before the testatrix died. The court held that this was initial failure and a fund can only be applied cy-près if there is proof of a general charitable intention shown by the testator. In this case there was a specific gift to a specific institution alone and the gift failed.

### CA Re Rymer [1895] 1 Ch 19

**Key Facts**

A legacy was left for St Thomas's Seminary in Westminister. It had closed down before the testator's death. There was no evidence of a general charitable intent.

### CA Biscoe v Jackson (1887) LR 35 Ch D 460

**Key Facts**

A gift was left to establish a soup kitchen and cottage hospital in Shoreditch. There was insufficient money to carry this out, but there was sufficient general charitable intent shown so the funds were transferred to benefit the poor of Shoreditch.

## 11.8.3 Subsequent failure of a charity

**Key Law**

Where a charitable gift fails because it ceases to exist or the charitable purpose becomes impossible to implement between the death of the testator and the administration of the estate by the executors it can be applied *cy-près* without the need to show a general charitable intent.

### CA Re Wright [1954] Ch 347

**Key Facts**

A testatrix left her residuary estate to a named person for life and then to be used for a convalescent home for impecunious gentlewomen. On the death of the tenant for life it was impracticable to provide a convalescent home. The court held it had already been dedicated to charity on the death of the settlor as it would then have been possible to set up the home.

## 11.8.4 Charities that have never existed

(HC) Re Harwood [1936] Ch 285

**Key Facts**

Funds were left for a list of charitable societies, including the Wisbech Peace Society which had ceased to exist before the testator's death, and the Peace Society of Belfast which had never existed. The gift to the institution which had ceased to exist failed, but the gift to the society which had never existed showed a general charitable intent and could be transferred under the *cy-près* doctrine.

## 11.8.5 Unincorporated charitable associations

(HC) Re Finger's Will Trusts [1972] Ch 286

**Key Facts**

The testatrix left a share of her estate to a number of charitable institutions including the National Radium Commission which was an unincorporated charity and the National Council for Maternity and Child Welfare which was an incorporated charity; both had ceased to exist. It was held that the gift to the unincorporated association could succeed because it was a gift for the purposes of the association, but the gift to the incorporated charity failed.

# 12

# Office of Trustee

## Appointment, retirement and removal of trustee

***Re Tempest (1866)***
The court should use certain criteria when appointing a new trustee including the wishes of the testator, the wishes of the beneficiaries and the effective administration of the trust

***Re Brockbank (1948)***
The court will not interfere with the appointment of a new trustee under s 36 of the Trustee Act 1925

***Re Stoneham's Settlement Trusts (1953)***
A trustee removed under s 36 is not a retiring trustee and cannot take part in decisions about his/her replacement

## Office of Trustee

## Management duties of trustees

***Speight v Gaunt (1883)***
A trustee is under a duty to act fairly and honestly and to take all precautions which an ordinary prudent man of business would take in managing similar affairs of his own

**DUTY TO INVEST THE TRUST PROPERTY**

***Nestle v NatWest Bank plc (1993)***
Trustees in breach of their investment duties could not be found liable for breach of trust unless their breaches could be directly linked to the loss arising to the trust

***Cowan v Scargill (1985)***
Trustees are under a duty to maximise the income from the trust and could not base investment decisions on moral choices

***Harries v Church Commissioners for England (1993)***
Ethical choices in investments could be justified for a religious charitable trust

## Duties of trustees

***Tempest v Lord Camoys (1882)***
Trustees must act unanimously when making decisions over the trust

**EXERCISE OF TRUSTEES' DISCRETION**

***Re Beloved Wilkes Charity (1851)***
Trustees do not have to give reasons for the choice of a discretionary beneficiary

***Scott v National Trust (1998)***
The trustees cannot be compelled to give reasons for the exercise of a discretion but they must explain any change in policy where the beneficiaries have a legitimate expectation that has arisen over a period of time

***Klug v Klug (1918)***
If trustees give reasons for the exercise of a discretion which are improper the court has the power to intervene

***Re Hastings-Bass (1975); Breadner v Granville-Grossman (2000)***
The court has the power to intervene in the exercise of a trustee's discretion only where the trustees fail to take into account something that they ought to have or failed to take into account something

**DISCLOSURE OF DOCUMENTS TO THE BENEFICIARIES**

***Abacus v Barr (2003)***
Where a court has the right to interfere with an appointment made under a discretion then a decision challenged successfully under the rule will be voidable and not void

***Re Londonderry's Settlement (1965)***
A beneficiary is not entitled to see documents which give reasons for the way in which the trustees had acted.

***O'Rourke v Darbishire (1920)***
A beneficiary is entitled to inspect documents related to the affairs of the trust

***Schmidt v Rosewood (2003)***
Beneficiaries under discretionary trusts and objects of a power of appointment have no right to see trust documents but can make a request to the court

# 12.1 Appointment, retirement and removal

## CA Re Tempest (1866) LR 1 Ch App 485

**Key Facts**

A successful challenge was made to the court's appointment of a new trustee under its statutory power on the basis that the trustee was a nominee of the beneficiary of the trust and he did not intend to act independently

**Key Law**

The court will use the following criteria when appointing a new trustee:

(i) they will have regard to the wishes of the testator;
(ii) they will have regard to the wishes of the beneficiaries;
(iii) they will have regard to the effective administration of the trust.

**Key Link**

Consider the court's appintment of trustees as part of its power to vary a settlement under VTA 1958; see **17.2**.

## HC Re Brockbank [1948] Ch 206

**Key Facts**

Where the power to appoint a trustee existed under s 36 Trustee Act 1925 then the court would not interfere with the appointment.

## HC Re Stoneham's Settlement Trusts [1953] Ch 59

**Key Facts**

A trustee had remained out of the jurisdiction for over 12 months and was removed by the other trustee under s 36 TA 1925.

**Key Law**

A trustee who is removed from the trust under s 36 TA 1925 is not retiring and therefore cannot take part in decisions about who is to be appointed to replace him.

# 12.2 Duties of trustees

## 12.2.1 Duty to act unanimously

(CA) Tempest v Lord Camoys (1882) 21 Ch D 571

**Key Facts**

One trustee refused to agree to the purchase of land. He was acting properly. It was held that trustees must act unanimously and the trustees could not act without his agreement.

## 12.2.2 Duty to exercise discretions properly

(CA) Re Beloved Wilkes Charity (1851) 3 Mac & G 440

**Key Facts**

Trustees had the power to select a boy to be educated as a priest in the Church of England with a preference within a certain area. They chose a boy outside the area. It was held that it was a proper choice and the trustees did not have to give reasons for their decision.

(HC) Scott v National Trust [1998] 2 All ER 705

**Key Facts**

The trustees of the National Trust without notice decided to withdraw the right to hunt over National Trust land. The court considered whether the trustees had to give reasons for the decision.

**Key Law**

Trustees could not be compelled to give reasons for the exercise of a discretion but where the beneficiaries had a legitimate expectation which had arisen over time then trustees had a duty to give them a reason for a change in policy.

## (HC) Klug v Klug [1918] 2 Ch 67

**Key Facts**

A mother who was trustee of a settlement under which her daughter was a beneficiary refused to exercise her discretionary power to advance capital to her daughter because she had married without her mother's consent.

The court held that where reasons were given for the exercise of a trustee's discretion and those reasons were improper then the court had power to intervene.

## (CA) Re Hastings-Bass [1975] Ch 25

**Key Facts**

Trustees were not aware that the exercise of their power of advancement to resettle property on trust for the purpose of avoiding estate duty power would make certain interests belonging to remainder beneficiaries void.

The court held it had the power to intervene even where the trustees had acted in good faith if it could be shown that the exercise of the discretion had produced a result which was clearly not intended by them.

## (HC) Breadner v Granville-Grossman [2000] 4 All ER 705

**Key Law**

The court has the power to interfere in the exercise of a trustee's discretion in the following circumstances:

(i) the trustees fail to take into account something which they ought to have taken into account; or

(ii) the trustees take into account something which they ought not to have taken into account; and

(iii) in either case the trustees would not have taken the action they had if they had not failed as in (i) to take into account what they ought to have taken into account, or had taken into account as in (ii) what they ought not to have taken into account.

These principles are based on earlier propositions first put forward in *Re Hastings-Bass (Dec'd)* [1975] Ch 25. This case is discussed **above**.

## (HC) Abacus Trust Company v Barr [2003] Ch 409

**Key Facts**

Trustees of a trust had mistakenly believed that the settlor had wanted the appointment of the fund to extend to 60 per cent of the fund, although he had only wanted it to extend to 40 per cent of the fund. This was a genuine misunderstanding.

**Key Law**

If the rule in *Hastings-Bass* concerning the exercise of the trustee's discretion has been breached then their decision is voidable and not void.

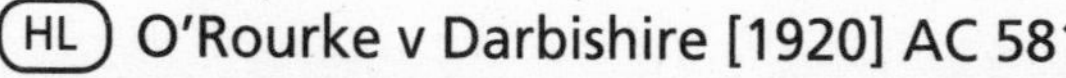

## (HL) O'Rourke v Darbishire [1920] AC 581

**Key Judgment**

**Lord Wrenbury:** 'The beneficiary is entitled to see all trust documents because they are trust documents and because he is a beneficiary. They are in this sense his own.'

## (CA) Re Londonderry's Settlement [1965] Ch 918

**Key Facts**

A beneficiary is entitled to see trust documents. These include any documentation concerning the administration of the trust but not documentation revealing the reasons for the trustees' decisions.

## (PC) Schmidt v Rosewood [2003] 2 WLR 1442

**Key Facts**

An object of a power of appointment sought disclosure of certain trusts documents including letters written by his father about the exercise of power.

The Privy Council held that he may have the right to disclosure of documents in the same way as the object of a discretionary trust, but it was a matter for the court's discretion as to whether disclosure would be exercised. They held that no beneficiary has a right to see any trust document, and it is always a matter for the court's discretion. This will depend on such issues as the likelihood of the claimant benefiting under the trust or power.

**Key Judgment**

**Lord Walker:** '... Their lordships consider that the more principled and correct approach is to regard the right to seek disclosure of trust documents as one aspect of the court's inherent jurisdiction to supervise, and if necessary intervene in, the administration of trusts. The right to seek the court's intervention does not depend on entitlement to a fixed and transmissible beneficial interest...'.

### Breakspear v Ackland [2009] Ch 32

**Key Facts**

Beneficiaries under a discretionary trust claimed the right to see a statement of wishes from the settlor concerning trust property. It was held that the trustees had a discretion to give such letters to the beneficiaries if they felt it was in the best interests of the trust.

**Key Law**

A beneficiary is not normally entitled to see any statement of wishes from a settlor of family property on discretionary trusts.

## 12.2.3 Management duties of trustees

**Key Comment**

Much of the control over the exercise of trustees duties is governed by statute, in particular the Trustee Act 1925 and the Trustee Act 2000. They have certain key duties including the duty to invest the trust funds.

### Speight v Gaunt (1883) 9 App Cas 1

**Key Law**

The general duty of a trustee is to act honestly and fairly and to take 'all those precautions which an ordinary prudent man of business would take in managing similar affairs of his own': Lord Blackburn.

## Nestle v National Westminister Bank plc [1993] 1 WLR 1260

**Key Facts**

The NatWest Bank acted as trustees to a settlement of the Nestle family. One of the beneficiaries claimed that if the bank had invested the fund properly it would have increased in value by four times.

The court held that although they had made errors of judgment, there had not been a breach of trust. They had failed to fully understand the extent of their investment powers and they had failed to review the investments, but these failures could not be directly linked to the loss to the beneficiary.

**Key Comment**

This decision suggests that it is very difficult for a beneficiary to successfully sue trustees for breach on the basis of investment decisions. However under the Trustee Act 2000 they would have been liable for a breach of their statutory duty of care and in particular their failure to review the investments, which is now a statutory duty.

## Cowan v Scargill [1985] Ch 270

**Key Facts**

Union trustees of the Pension Fund for the National Union of Mineworkers challenged the investment policy of the pension fund, which included investments in overseas industries in direct competition with the United Kingdom coal industry. It was held that the duty of trustees is to optimise the benefits which the beneficiaries are to receive, and in general, financial considerations would prevail over ethical considerations.

**Key Judgment**

**Sir Robert Megarry:** 'Trustees may have strongly held social or political views. They may be firmly opposed to any investments in South Africa or other countries or they may object to any form of investment in companies concerned with alcohol, tobacco, armaments or other controversial products … if investments of this kind would be more beneficial to the beneficiaries than other investments, the trustees must not refrain from making the investments by reason of the views that they hold.'

### Harries v Church Commissioners for England [1993] 2 All ER 300

**Key Facts**

The Church Commissioners' investment policy was based on ethical considerations, which meant they chose not to invest in some high profit yielding investments such as gambling and the tobacco industry. This policy was upheld by the courts, since it could be justified for a religious charity whose members were likely to support such a policy.

**Key Law**

Trustees are under a duty to maximise their investments for their beneficiaries but some charitable institutions were entitled to operate an ethical investment policy.

## 12.2.4 Investment

**Key Comment**

The Trustee Act 2000 lays down statutory duties with regard to investment including the standard investment criteria which impose a duty on trustees to consider the suitability of investments and to ensure that they are sufficiently diversified. They also have a duty to review the investments from time to time and a duty to take advice where appropriate.

# 13

# Breach of Trust

## Breach of Trust

### Trustees Liability

**Investments**

***Fry v Fry (1859)***

A trustee who improperly retains an unauthorised investment will be liable for the difference between the actual selling price and the price it would have raised if it had been sold at the proper time

***Bartlett v Barclay's Bank Trust Co Ltd (1980)***

Trustees were not entitled to set off a loss incurred on one transaction against a gain on another project

### Exemption Clauses

***Armitage v Nurse (1998)***

There is an irreducible core of obligations of duties owed by the trustees to the beneficiaries which cannot be exempted by the trustees.

***Walker v Stones (2000)***

Trustees cannot exempt themselves from something that no reasonable solicitor trustee could have thought was for the benefit of the trust

### Liability for breach of trust

***Target Holdings v Redferns (1995)***

If the claimant can show that the loss would not have occurred but for the breach then the trustee would be liable

### Defences of a trustee

**Indemnity against a co-trustee**

***Bahin v Hughes (1886)***

Trustees are jointly and severally liable for a breach of trust and cannot claim to be indemnified because they have not taken an active role in the breach of trust

***Head v Gould (1898)***

A lay trustee can claim to be indemnified against a professional trustee if the other trustee has exercised such a degree of influence over the other trustee that the other trustee has been unable to exercise an independent judgment

**Beneficiaries consent**

***Re Pauling's Settlement Trusts (1964)***

Trustees would not be liable for a beach of trust where the beneficiaries had expressly given their consent

**s 61 Trustee Act 1925**

***Bartlett v Barclay's Bank (1980)***

s 61 cannot be used where the trustees have acted negligently and cannot claim to have acted reasonably

# 13.1 Exemption clauses

## CA Armitage v Nurse [1998] Ch 241

**Key Facts**

A clause inserted into a trust deed which exempted the trustees from liability for any loss whatsoever 'unless such loss or damage shall be caused by his own actual fraud' was upheld.

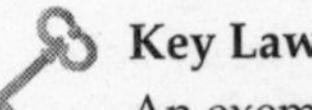

**Key Law**

An exemption clause will exempt trustees from liability for any breach unless it arises through dishonesty. Dishonesty was defined as when a trustee acts in a way which he does not honestly believe is in the beneficiaries' interests and it is none the less dishonest because he does not intend to benefit himself.

**Key Judgment**

**Millett LJ:** 'I accept … that there is an irreducible core of obligations owed by the trustees to the beneficiaries and enforceable by them which is fundamental to the concept of a trust. If the beneficiaries have no rights enforceable against the trustees there are no trusts. But I do not accept the further submission that these core obligations include the duties of skill and care, prudence and diligence. The duty of trustees to perform the trusts honestly and in good faith for the benefit of the beneficiaries is the minimum necessary to give substance to the trusts, but in my opinion it is sufficient…'.

## CA Walker v Stones [2000] 4 All ER 412

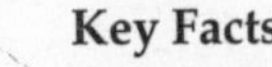

**Key Facts**

A trust instrument had included an exclusion clause which purported to exempt a solicitor-trustee from liability for wilful fraud or dishonesty. The issue was how far this clause would exempt a trustee from a breach of trust. It was held that there must be an objective standard in assessing what the trustee could have genuinely believed. They could not be exempt from something that no reasonable solicitor trustee could have thought that what he did or agreed to do was for the benefit of the trust.

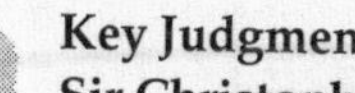

**Key Judgment**

**Sir Christopher Slade:** 'That clause in my judgment would not exempt the trustee from liability for breaches of trust, even if committed in the genuine belief that the course taken was in the best interests of the beneficiaries, if such belief was so unreasonable that no reasonable solicitor trustee could have held that belief.'

**Key Comment**

A recent Law Commission report on exemption clauses rejects a total prohibition on their use but suggests that there should be greater control over the content of such clauses. There should also be a distinction between the use of exemption clauses by professional and lay trustees. However rather than control through legislation, control should come from a Code of Practice.

## 13.2 The meaning of breach of trust

**Key Law**

If a trustee acts in a manner that is inconsistent with the terms of the trust he/she will have committed a breach of trust.

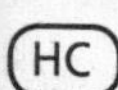

Bartlett v Barclay's Bank Co Ltd [1980] Ch 515

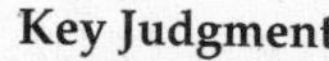

**Key Judgment**

'… It is the duty of a trustee to conduct the business of the trust with the same care as an ordinary prudent man of business would extend towards his own affairs.'

## 13.3 Remedy for breach of trust

### 13.3.1 Nature of liability for breach of trust

**Key Law**

Where a trustee causes a loss to the trust fund or trust estate he will be personally liable to replace the loss although a trustee will only be liable for his own breaches of trust

## 13.3.2 Trustees are jointly and severally liable for breaches of trust

### CA Bishopsgate Investment Management Ltd v Maxwell (No 2) [1994] 1 AER 261

**Key Facts**

Two brothers, Kevin and Ian Maxwell both signed transfers of assets wrongly transferring them from pension funds for employees of their company. Both were held to be jointly and severally liable for breach of trust although one brother said he was unaware of what he was doing because he had signed blank transfers.

## 13.3.3 Causation in breach of trust

**Key Law**

If there is no causal link between the breach and the loss the trustee will not be liable.

### HL Target Holdings v Redferns [1995] 3 All ER 785

**Key Facts**

£1.525 million was lent by the claimant mortgagees Target Holdings to a company to be secured on property which had been fraudulently made to appear to be worth £2 million, but in reality was worth £775,000. The defendants Redferns were a firm of solicitors and were not party to the fraud but acted for both the purchasers and the mortgagees. The purchasers became insolvent and the property was repossessed by the mortgagees, the claimants. The claimants sued the solicitors for the shortfall between the money lent and the actual value of the property.

It was held that although the solicitors had acted in breach of trust by paying out the mortgage funds without authority, they were not liable for the loss because it was not caused by the defendants. If the claimants had advanced the same amount of money they would have got the same security with or without the breach of trust by the defendants.

**Key Law**

Lord Browne-Wilkinson was concerned that the rules developed from traditional trusts should not be applied in the setting of a commercial trust. However where the claimant can show that the loss would not have occurred but for the breach then the trustee would be liable for the total loss irrespective if the immediate cause of the loss was connected with a third party. This is because the common law rules of remoteness and causation do not apply.

**Key Judgment**

**Lord Browne-Wilkinson:** '… there does have to be some causal link between the breach of trust and the loss to the trust estate for which compensation is recoverable, viz the fact that the loss would not have occurred but for the breach.'

## 13.4 Investments

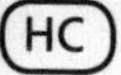

### Fry v Fry (1859) 27 Beav 144

**Key Facts**

Trustees of an estate advertised a property for sale at £1,000 in 1836 and refused an offer one year later of £900. A railway opened in 1843 and custom was affected, and when the property was advertised again in 1845 no offers were made. The trustees were held liable for the difference between the offer in 1837 and the actual sum received in 1859.

**Key Law**

A trustee who improperly retains an unauthorised investment will be liable for the difference between the actual selling price and the price which it would have raised if it had been sold at the proper time.

### Bartlett v Barclays Bank Trust Co. Ltd (No 1) [1980] Ch 515

**Key Facts**

The trust property of a trust consisted largely of shares in a private property company and the trustees were professional trustees. The company decided that it would invest in some speculative property deals. One, called the Guildford project, was a success, but the second, called the Old Bailey project, was a disaster and resulted in a loss. It was held that the losses in the Old Bailey project could be set off against the gains made in the Guildford project.

**Key Law**

Generally where the trustees in breach of trust make a profit on one transaction and a loss on another they are not allowed to set off the loss against the profit, unless the profit and the loss are treated as part of a single transaction.

**Key Judgment**

**Brightman J:** 'I think it would be unjust to deprive the bank of the element of salvage in the course of assessing the cost of the shipwreck.'

## 13.5 Indemnity against a co-trustee

### Bahin v Hughes (1886) 31 Ch D 390

**Key Facts**

A passive trustee sought an indemnity against a fellow trustee, who had invested funds in an unauthorised investment.

**Key Law**

Trustees are jointly and severally liable for a breach of trust and cannot claim to be indemnified because they have not taken an active role in the breach of trust.

**Key Judgment**

**Cotton LJ:** 'Miss Hughes was the active trustee and Mr Edwards did nothing and in my opinion it would be laying down a wrong rule that where one trustee acts honestly though erroneously the other trustee is to be held entitled to indemnity who by doing nothing neglects his duty more than the acting trustee…'.

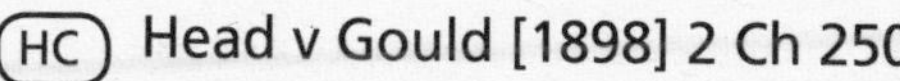

## HC Head v Gould [1898] 2 Ch 250

**Key Facts**

A solicitor and a beneficiary were appointed as trustees of a trust. A number of breaches of trust occurred and the lay trustee claimed to be indemnified by her co-trustee. The court found that she was aware of the circumstances of the breaches of trust and had actively encouraged her co-trustee to commit the breach of trust. They held that she could not claim an indemnity from her co-trustee.

**Key Law**

A lay trustee can claim to be indemnified where one trustee is a solicitor and has exercised such a degree of influence over the other trustee that the other trustee has been unable to exercise an independent judgment.

**Key Judgment**

**Kekewich J:** 'A man is not bound to indemnify his co-trustee against loss merely because he was a solicitor, when that co-trustee was an active participator in the breach of trust complained of, and is not proved to have participated merely in consequence of the advice and control of the solicitor.'

**Key Comment**

The rule in *Chillingworth v Chambers* lays down that where a trustee who is also a beneficiary participates in a breach of trust, he may not claim a share in the trust estate until he has made good his liability as trustee. The beneficiary trustee must indemnify his co-trustee to the extent of his beneficial interest. However if the loss exceeds the beneficial interest, the trustees will share the excess loss equally between them.

# 13.6 Defences

## 13.6.1 Beneficiaries' consent

## CA Re Pauling's Settlement Trusts [1964] Ch 303

**Key Facts**

A marriage settlement created in 1919 included an express provision that the trustees could advance up to one-half of the beneficiaries' presumptive share under the trust for their advancement or absolute use. Advances had been made by the trustees, who were the bank Coutts & Co. The beneficiaries sued the trustees for breach of trust in advancing the shares to the beneficiaries when the money had generally been paid not to them but into their mother's bank account. The court held that the trustees were not liable because the beneficiaries were all of age and had consented to the advances.

**Key Law**

A beneficiary can only consent if he/she is of full age and is not under any other incapacity.

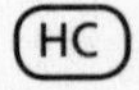



## Bartlett v Barclays Bank [1980] (above)

**Key Facts**

A bank had been held liable for failing to supervise two land development projects by a company where the bank held 99.8 per cent of its shares as trustees for the Bartlett Trust. The investment had proved to be unsuitable. The bank claimed a defence under s 61, claiming that they had acted reasonably under s 61 Trustee Act 1925. The defence was rejected because they were found to be negligent and could not then claim to have acted reasonably.

# 13.6.2 s 61 Trustee Act 1925

**Key Law**

Section 61 of the Trustee Act 1925 confers a discretion on the court to relieve a trustee wholly or partly for a breach of trust

# 13.6.3 Limitation Act 1980

**Key Law**

A beneficiary must bring an action for breach of trust within the prescribed limitation period which is SIX YEARS (s 21(3)Limitation Act 1980). There is no limitation period for actions based on fraud or where a trustee retains trust property.

**Key Comment**

The Law Commission has proposed reform of the rules on limitation because they are out of date and often unfair. It proposes that there should no longer be a distinction between different causes of action but instead one basic core limitation period of three years from when the claimant becomes aware of the facts giving rise to the cause of action.

14

# Breach of Fiduciary Duty

***Bray v Ford (1896)***
It is an inflexible rule of a court of equity that a person in a fiduciary position is not allowed to put himself in a position where his interest and his duty conflict

## Types of fiduciary relationship

***A-G v Blake (1998)***
A fiduciary relationship did not continue after a former secret agent left the government
***Reading v Att-Gen (1951)***
Profits made in breach of a fiduciary relationship must be accounted to the principal
***Regal Hastings Ltd v Gulliver (1967)***
Company directors are in a fiduciary position and must account to the company for any personal profits made
***Industrial Developments Consultants Ltd v Cooley (1972)***
A fiduciary must not place himself in a position where his duty and interest conflict
***Queensland Mines Ltd v Hudson (1978)***
Where a fiduciary acts with the full knowledge and consent of his/her principal and the fiduciary relationship has ended, then the fiduciary can retain profits made through the relationship
***Sinclair Invesment Holding SA v Versailles Trade Finance Ltd (2005)***
***Daraydan Holdings Ltd v Solland International Ltd (2005)***

## Incidental profits

***Keech v Sandford (1726)***
A trustee cannot keep for himself a renewal of a lease which he was able to obtain for himself by reason of his being the trustee of the original lease
***Re Macadam (1946)***
If a trustee acquires a directorship through his/her position as trustee remuneration received must be accounted to the trust
**Bribes**
***Lister v Stubbs (1890)***
Bribes received by the foreman of a company were not held on constructive trust and so although the money had to be returned profits made with the money could be retained
***Att-Gen for Hong Kong v Reid (1994)***
Bribes received by a fiduciary were held on constructive trust
***Imageview Management Ltd v Jack (2009)***

## Liability for breach of fiduciary duty

***Boardman v Phipps (1967)***
A fiduciary will be held strictly liable to account for any profits made wherever it can be said that his/her duty and interest conflict. No distinction is made between an honest and a dishonest trustee. The court can award compensation where a fiduciary has acted honestly and in the best interests of the trust
***Cobbetts v Hodge (2009)***
The award of compensation to a fiduciary who has to account for profits but has acted honestly is at the discretion of the court

## Purchase of trust property by the trustees

***Holder v Holder (1968)***
A sale will not be set aside where there is no conflict of interest

## Competition with the trust

***Re Thomson (1903)***
A trustee in direct competition with the trust must account for any profits made

## Remuneration

***Williams v Barton (1927)***
Any unauthorised commission received by the trustees must be accounted to the trust
***O'Sullivan v Management Agency and Music Ltd (1985)***
Profits made on a contract which was set aside on the grounds of undue influence had to be accounted for but reasonable remuneration could be awarded

### HL Bray v Ford [1896] AC 44

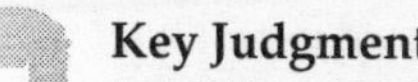

**Key Judgment**

**Lord Herschell:** 'It is an inflexible rule of a Court of Equity that a person in a fiduciary position … is not, unless otherwise expressly provided, entitled to make a profit; he is not allowed to put himself into a position where his interest and his duty conflict…'.

### LAC Minerals v International Corona Ltd (1989) 61 DLR (4th) (Supreme Court of Canada)

**Key Judgment**

'There are few legal concepts more frequently invoked but less conceptually certain than that of the fiduciary relationship...'

# 14.1 The nature of a fiduciary relationship

## 14.1.1 Types of fiduciary relationships

### CA Att-Gen v Blake [1998] 1 All ER 833

**Key Facts**

Blake was a former secret agent who received confidential information. He later wrote about his life as an agent and the Crown claimed that the publication of the book was in breach of his fiduciary duty. It was held that although he had been in a fiduciary relationship formerly, that relationship ended after he left the employment of the UK Government.

### HL Reading v Att-Gen [1951] AC 507

**Key Facts**

A sergeant in the British army used his position to enable civilians to pass through checkpoints with smuggled goods.

**Key Law**

It was held that he was in a fiduciary relationship and must account to the Crown the profits that he had wrongly made through the misuse of his position.

## 14.1.2 Company directors and fiduciary duties in the commercial context

### (HL) Regal (Hastings) Ltd v Gulliver [1967] 2 AC 134

**Key Facts**

Four company directors of R Ltd personally subscribed for shares in a subsidiary company because R Ltd did not have the requisite money available. The directors were held liable to account to the company for the profits made from their personal shareholding.

**Key Law**

A fiduciary must account for any profit made through his position although he has acted bona fide throughout.

### (HC) Industrial Developments Consultants Ltd v Cooley [1972] 1 WLR 443

**Key Facts**

The defendant was employed by the claimant company, which offered construction consultancy services. He entered into negotiations with the Gas Board on their behalf but the negotiations broke down. He then left the company having told them that he was ill, and went to work for the Gas Board himself. It was held that he had to account for the profits he gained to his employers. His employers would not have released him if they had been aware of the full facts.

**Key Law**

A fiduciary must not place himself in a position where his duty and his interest conflict.

### (PC) Queensland Mines Ltd v Hudson (1978) 18 ALR 1

**Key Facts**

The defendant, who was the managing director of a company, successfully obtained mining licences on its behalf. When the company did not proceed he resigned as managing director and proceeded, several years later, with the full knowledge of the company with the mining venture himself. It was held that he did not have to account for the profits to the company.

**Key Law**

Where a fiduciary acts with the full knowledge and consent of his principal, then the fiduciary is entitled to retain profits made through his position.

**Key Problem**

In this case, could it be argued that consent should have come from the shareholders and not from the board?

### CA Sinclair Investment Holding SA v Versailles Trade Finance Ltd [2005] EWCA Civ 722

**Key Facts**

Versailles Trade Finance was part of a larger group in which the defendant had a substantial interest. He was able to make a large profit and thereby repay a mortgage on a property which he sold for £8.6 million because the group falsely inflated its turnover through some dishonest dealings. The claimant argued the defendant owed him a fiduciary duty which had been breached and claimed this profit. The defendant argued that since he did not hold legal title over the claimant's monies no such relationship could arise. However the court found that the Versailles Group had agreed an express term that monies would be held on trust for the claimant if not used for trading.

## 14.2 Purchase of trust property by the trustees

### CA Holder v Holder [1968] Ch 353

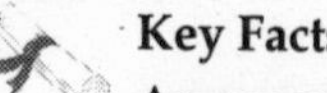

**Key Facts**

An executor, the son of the deceased, purchased trust property at a public auction after renouncing his executorship. Unknown to him, he was technically regarded as an executor because he had undertaken some executor duties. The sale was not set aside, because he had never assumed the duties of an executor and there was no conflict of interest.

**Key Law**

The self-dealing rule applies when a trustee purchases trust property from the trust. It prevents a trustee from purchasing trust property even where it is at public auction and at a fair price. The transaction is voidable by a beneficiary.

## 14.3 Incidental profits

### 14.3.1 Purchase of a lease

HC Keech v Sandford (1726) Sel Cas Ch 61

**Key Facts**

A trustee held the profits of a lease of Romford market on trust for a child. He asked the landlord to renew the lease and he refused to grant the lease to the child, because he felt he had no rights of enforcement against a child because he was a minor. The trustee then renewed the lease in his own name. It was held that the trustee must hold the lease on trust for the child, and account for any profits he made.

**Key Law**

A trustee cannot keep for his own benefit a renewal of a lease which he was able to obtain for himself by reason of his being the trustee of the original lease.

### 14.3.2 Remuneration received as a director

HC Re Macadam [1946] Ch 73

**Key Facts**

Trustees had the power to appoint two directors of a company, and they chose to appoint themselves. It was held that they must account to the trust for the remuneration that they received.

**Key Law**

If trustees acquire their position as directors through the trust, then they are accountable to the trust for any remuneration that they receive.

## (HC) Re Gee [1948] Ch 284

**Key Facts**

The trust held a shareholding which gave it votes in the election of a director. In this case the trustee could show that he would have become trustee even if all the trust votes had been used against him.

**Key Comment**

If the trustee can show that he/she became trustee without relying on the votes of the trust, then he is entitled to retain the remuneration received. Compare the cases of *Re Macadam* and *Re Gee*. A trustee is also able to retain remuneration received where his appointment to the directorship was before he became trustee (*Re Dover Coalfield Extension* [1908] 1 Ch 65).

# 14.3.3 Bribes

## (CA) Lister v Stubbs (1890) 45 Ch D 1

**Key Facts**

The foreman of a company received money by way of bribes. He acted as agent for the company, awarding contracts to competing companies. Although he had to account for the money received, he did not have to account for the profit he made by investing the money.

**Key Comment**

In this case the courts granted a personal remedy only based on the relationship of creditor and debtor. They held that the money he received was not held on constructive trust. The decision was subject to criticism, but it took over 100 years for the decision to be overturned.

## Att-Gen for Hong Kong v Reid [1994] 1 AC 324

**Key Facts**

The defendant was employed as a public prosecutor for the Hong Kong government. He received substantial bribes in the course of his job. Part of the money was used to purchase three properties in New Zealand. It was found that he held the money as a constructive trustee, and therefore it could be traced into the houses in New Zealand.

**Key Law**

This case reverses the decision in *Lister v Stubbs*, although it is a decision of the Privy Council and is strictly obiter. It is likely to be followed in later cases.

HC Daraydan Holdings Ltd v Solland International Ltd [2005] 4 AER 73

**Key Judgment**

**Lawrence Collins J:** 'There are powerful policy reasons for ensuring that a fiduciary does not retain gains acquired in violation of fiduciary duty, and I do not consider that it should make any difference whether the fiduciary is insolvent. There is no injustice to the creditors in their not sharing in an asset for which the fiduciary has not given value, and which the fiduciary should not have had.'

## 14.3.4 Competition with trust

HC Re Thomson [1903] 1 Ch 203

**Key Facts**

A trustee of a yacht broking business set up independently as a yacht broker. It was held that he had to account for any profits he received to the trust, because he was in breach of his fiduciary duty.

**Key Law**

If the trustee forms a business which is similar but not in direct competition with the trust then the trustee does not have to account for any profits he receives.

CA Imageview Management Ltd v Jack [2009] EWCA Civ 63

**Key Facts**

The defendant was a footballer who wanted to work in the UK and needed a work permit. He hired an agent and agreed to pay 10 per cent of his salary to him for his work in negotiating a contract for the footballer with Dundee United. The club agreed to pay the agent a sum of £3,000 in commission in order to get a work permit for the footballer costing £750. The footballer claimed that he was entitled to the commission received by the agent from the club.

**Key Law**

The defendant's claim was upheld on the basis that the commission received by the agent from the club was a secret profit and was a breach of the agent's duty of good faith owed to his principal. Once a conflict of interest was proved the agent lost his/her right to remuneration.

**Key Comment**

The court has a discretion to reward the fiduciary who has made a profit for the trust as well as himself as discussed below under *Boardman v Phipps*. In this case compensation was refused because the agent had acted surreptitiously.

## 14.4 Liability for breach of fiduciary duty

### Boardman v Phipps [1967] 2 AC 46

**Key Facts**

Boardman was a solicitor to the trust and he and another beneficiary were dissatisfied with the way the company was run. Boardman personally acquired a majority shareholding using knowledge he had gained from the trust in order to gain control of the company. Some of the beneficiaries were informed of his actions but the elderly widow was unable to give consent as she was senile. The company became profitable and both Boardman and the trust profited. It was held that any personal profit made by Boardman was held on constructive trust for the beneficiaries. Unusually the court held that he should be rewarded by the payment of a *quantum meruit* because at all times he had acted *bona fides* and in the best interests of the trust.

**Key Law**

A fiduciary will be held strictly liable to account for any profits made, wherever it can be said that his duty and interest conflict. The law does not distinguish between the dishonest and the honest trustee; both must account for any profit made by virtue of their position. Until *Att-Gen for Hong Kong v Reid*, the law seemed to favour the dishonest fiduciary making a profit from his position. Reconsider the decision in *Lister v Stubbs* above.

### HC Cobbetts v Hodge [2009] EWHC 786

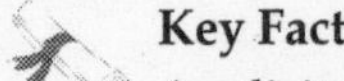

**Key Facts**

A solicitor purchased shares using knowledge he had acquired whilst working for the claimants, a firm of solicitors. The claimants argued that the profit and the shares were held on constructive trust for them, arguing that the shares had been purchased whilst he was in their employment and were therefore purchased in breach of his duty of loyalty to them. The court held that the shares were held on constructive trust for the solicitors.

## 14.5 Remunerationion

### CA Re Duke of Norfolk's Settlement Trusts [1982] Ch 61

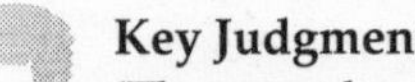

**Key Judgment**

'The court has to balance two influences which are to some extent in conflict. The first is that the office of trustee is, as such, gratuitous; the court will … be careful to protect the interests of the beneficiaries against claims by the trustees. The second is that it is of great importance to the beneficiaries that the trust should be well-administered… .'

## 14.5.1 Unauthorised remuneration

### HC Williams v Barton [1927] 2 Ch 9

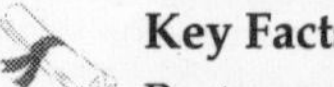

**Key Facts**

Barton was one of two trustees. He worked for a firm of stockbrokers. He persuaded his co-trustee to use his firm for work in connection with the trust. He received commission for this, and it was held that he must account to the trust for this.

## 14.5.2 Authorised remuneration

### O'Sullivan v Management Agency and Music Ltd [1985] QB 428

**Key Facts**

A contract between a musician and a management company had been set aside on the grounds of undue influence. It was held that the company had to account for the profits made under the contract, but the agent was awarded reasonable remuneration for the work carried out.

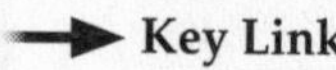

**Key Link**

See *Boardman v Phipps* above.

# 15

# Tracing

## Tracing at common law

***Foskett v McKeown (2001)***
*'Following is the process of following the same asset from hand to hand. Tracing is the process of identifying a new asset as a substitute for the old'*
***Taylor v Plumer (1815)***
Property can be traced at common law where there has been a clean substitution of the property and it has not been mixed with other property
***Boscawen v Bajwa (1996)***
Monies lent for the redemption of a mortgage and used for other purposes could be traced through subrogation into the hands of the purchaser who had been unjustly enriched at the expense of the mortgagees
***Trustee of the property of FC Jones and son (a firm) v Jones (1996)***
A claimant could trace into property at common law and was entitled to claim any profit derived from that profit
***Banque Belge pour L'etranger v Hambrouck (1921)***
There can be common law tracing into a bank account if the funds have not been mixed with other moneys

## Tracing

## Tracing in equity

***Re Hallet's Estate (1880)***
Where a trustee or fiduciary has mixed funds with those of his own then he is deemed to use his own money first and the beneficiaries are entitled to a charge on the fund to satisfy their claim
***Space Investments Ltd v Canadian Imperial Bank of Commerce Trust Co (1986)***
The right to trace was dependent on proof that the trustees were in breach of trust or breach of fiduciary duty
***Foskett v McKeown (2001)***
A claimant in equity is entitled to either claim a proportionate share of the asset or to enforce a lien over it
***Re Oatway (1903)***
The beneficiaries' claim must first be satisfied from any identifiable part of the mixed fund before the trustees could claim any part of it for him/herself.
***Re Tilley's Wills Trust (1967)***
The beneficiaries have the choice whether to claim a charge over the asset or to claim for a proportional increase in the value of the asset
***Roscoe v Winder (1915)***
It is only possible to trace into the lowest intermediate balance left in the account
***Re Goldcorp (1994)***
Assets which have not been segregated from the whole cannot be traced
***Bishopsgate Investment Management Ltd v Homan (1994)***
There can be no backwards tracing into a fund unless it can be shown that a loan was always going to be repaid with the misappropriated money
***Clayton's Case (1816)***
The first money in will be deemed to be the first money out in a current account comprising money of an innocent volunteer and/or two or more trust accounts
***Barlow Clowes International Ltd and Others v Vaughan and others (1992) Re Diplock (1948)***
The 'first in first out' rule in Clayton's case can be ignored where it would cause injustice and the court were entitled to apply *pari passu*

# 15.1 What is tracing?

## (HL) Foskett v McKeown [2001] 1 AC 102

**Key Facts**

**Lord Millett:** 'Following is the process of following the same asset as it moves from hand to hand. Tracing is the process of identifying a new asset as the substitute for the old…'.

# 15.2 Tracing at common law

## (CA) Taylor v Plumer (1815) 3 M & S 562

**Key Facts**

Sir Thomas Plumer gave a sum of money to Walsh, his stockbroker, expressly to be invested in Exchequer bonds. Walsh used the money to purchase American bonds and bullion. Ownership in the American bonds and the bullion was disputed between Plumer and Walsh's trustee in bankruptcy. The property was held to belong to Plumer.

**Key Law**

Property can be traced at common law where there has been a clean substitution of the property and it has not been mixed with any other property.

**Key Judgment**

**Lord Ellenborough:** 'It makes no difference in reason or law into what other form, different from the original, the change may have been made … for the product or the substitute for the original thing still follows the nature of the thing itself…'.

## (CA) Boscawen v Bajwa [1996] 1 WLR 328 CA

**Key Facts**

A building society advanced money for the purchase of property and also for the discharge of the first legal charge on that property. The society intended to have a first legal charge on completion. The moneys were advanced but were not used to discharge the existing charge. However it was held that the building society could claim to be subrogated to the position of the original legal chargee.

**Key Law**

It was held to be unconscionable on behalf of the purchaser that the charge had been redeemed for the purchaser's benefit.

**Key Comment**

The principle of unjust enrichment was applied because the building society based their claim on the law of restitution. The issue was whether the second chargee would be unjustly enriched at the claimant's expense in the absence of such subrogation. The key issue here was that the building society had always intended to take out a charge over the property, and never to take out an unsecured loan.

## Banque Belge pour L'Etranger v Hambrouck [1921] 1 KB 321

**Key Facts**

A man unlawfully obtained cheques from his employer and paid them into his bank account. The money was then passed to his mistress, who in turn paid it into her own bank account. It was held that the money could be traced at common law into her account.

**Key Law**

There was nothing to prevent tracing at common law into a bank account if the funds had not been mixed with other moneys.

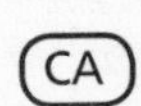

## Trustee of the Property of FC Jones and Son (a firm) v Jones [1996] 3 WLR 703

**Key Facts**

One partner in a firm of potato growers took £11,700 from the partnership and transferred it to his wife who used it to purchase potato futures, which increased in value to £50,760. The partnership was adjudicated bankrupt and the trustee in bankruptcy claimed he was entitled to both the sum taken from the partnership account as well as the profit generated. The trustee in bankruptcy could trace the whole sum at common law. There had been no mixing of the fund in the bank account.

**Key Law**

Once the claimant could show he/she was entitled to the property at common law then he/she would be entitled not only to trace the property into any exchange product, but also to trace any profit made from it.

**Key Problem**

If Mrs Jones had had £1 of her own money in the account, then there would have been no right to trace at common law. There would have been no right to trace in equity either, because there was no fiduciary relationship between the trustee in bankruptcy and Mrs Jones.

## 15.3 Tracing in equity

### 15.3.1 When does it arise?

CA Re Hallett's Estate (1880) 13 Ch D 696

**Key Facts**

Mr Hallett was a solicitor. He mixed funds from a trust with his own personal money in a money account. On his death there was insufficient money in his account to pay his debts and to return the money in full to the trust.

**Key Law**

Where a trustee or fiduciary has mixed his funds with that of the beneficiary, or has purchased further property with a mixed fund the following principles apply:

(i) the beneficiaries are entitled to a charge on the fund in order to satisfy their claim;

(ii) if a trustee withdraws money for his own purposes he is deemed to draw out his own money first, so that the beneficiaries can claim the fund as against the general creditors.

## Space Investments Ltd v Canadian Imperial Bank of Commerce Trust Co [1986] 1 WLR 1072

**Key Facts**

A bank was trustee of various settlements. The trust instrument included a provision that allowed the bank as trustee to borrow money from itself. The bank borrowed money as it was legally entitled to do and then became insolvent. The beneficiaries unsuccessfully claimed the right to trace into the overdrawn bank accounts and thereby to gain priority over the other creditors because there was no surviving asset into which they could trace; therefore the claims of the beneficiaries only ranked as unsecured creditors.

**Key Law**

The Privy Council refused them the right to do so. Such a right could only arise if the trustees had been in breach of trust.

## (HL) Foskett v McKeown (2001) (above)

**Key Facts**

Mr Murphy held over £2.7 million as trustee for various investors in a property development scheme in Portugal but the land was purchased and never developed. The funds of the investors were dissipated and were used partly to pay premiums towards a life insurance policy for £1 million taken out on Mr Murphy's life in 1986. He paid the first three premiums but in breach of trust the investor's funds were used to pay the remaining two premiums in 1989 and 1990. Mr Murphy committed suicide in 1991 and the insurance company paid out £1 million. Mr McKeown acted on behalf of the investors who claimed that they should be able to claim a share in the monies from the life insurance policy.

**Key Law**

At first instance Laddie J held that the claimants were entitled to a lien on the proceeds equivalent to their contribution, which was 54.46 per cent.

The Court of Appeal held the claimants were only entitled to recover the premiums paid with their money, amounting to approximately £20,000.

The House of Lords, reinstating the decision of the court at first instance, held that the depositors could trace into the premiums paid as the money had been used to purchase an asset (the policy) and then into the chose in action which was the policy and then into the proceeds of the insurance policy.

**Key Judgment**

**Lord Millett:** 'Where a trustee wrongfully uses trust money to provide part of the cost of acquiring an asset, the beneficiary is entitled at his option either to claim a proportionate share of the asset or to enforce a lien upon it to secure his personal claim against the trustee for the amount of the misapplied money. It does not matter whether the trustee mixed the trust money with his own in a single fund before using it to acquire the asset, or made separate payments out of the differently owned funds to acquire a single asset.'

**Key Problem**

It was assumed that the reason why the investors were successful was because the proceeds could not be paid unless all the premiums were paid, but this was not true since the money was payable on the receipt of one premium only. However, if Mr McKeown had failed to pay all the premiums then the insurance company would not have been bound to honour the policy.

## 15.4 Key issues arising in tracing in equity

### 15.4.1 Rights in an asset purchased by the trustee

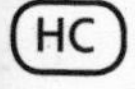

Re Oatway [1903] 2 Ch 356

**Key Facts**

A trustee withdrew funds from a mixed bank account and invested it. He then withdrew the remaining funds in the account and dissipated it. The beneficiaries could claim rights in the asset purchased by the trustee.

**Key Law**

The beneficiaries' claim must first be satisfied from any identifiable part of the mixed fund before the trustee could claim any part of it for him/herself.

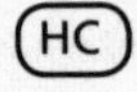

## Turner v Jacob [2006] EWHC 1317

**Key Judgment**

'... where the trustee maintains in the account an amount equal to the remaining trust fund, the beneficiary's right to trace is limited to that fund. It is not open to the beneficiary to assert a lien against an investment made using monies out of the mixed fund unless the sum expended is of such a size that it must have included trust monies ... .'

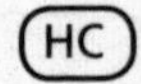

## Re Tilley's Wills Trust [1967] Ch 1179

**Key Facts**

Small sums from a trust fund had been paid into a bank account by an executrix of an estate. The executrix herself had a life interest. She had used these funds along with an overdraft facility at the bank, to purchase property, which had increased in value. On her death the increase in value of the properties was claimed by those entitled to the estate. The court held that the trust money had not been used for the purchase of the property but instead it had been used towards the reduction of the overdraft. The beneficiaries were only entitled to the return of their money with interest.

**Key Law**

Where a trustee uses trust monies to purchase an asset then the beneficiaries are entitled to choose either to claim a charge over the asset or to a claim for the proportional increase in the value of the asset.

**Key Comment**

This case clearly states that it is not possible to trace into an overdrawn bank account because the payment merely goes towards a reduction in the overdraft which is itself a debt owed to the bank. Where property is used to discharge a debt the law holds it has been dissipated as there is no asset remaining that could constitute the beneficiaries' property.

## 15.4.2 Lowest intermediate balance

### HC Roscoe v Winder [1915] 1 Ch 62

**Key Facts**

A purchaser of a business agreed to return a sum of money to the vendor company. This was recovered and partly paid into the purchaser's bank account. Most of the sum was dissipated, leaving only £25 in the account. Further monies were paid into the account. The company claimed the full balance in the account, which would cover over half of what was owed to them.

**Key Law**

It was held that the charge over the account was restricted to the lowest intermediate balance left in the account before subsequent monies were added and in this case it was £25 only.

## 15.4.3 Assets must first be segregated for a proprietary claim to subsist

### PC Re Goldcorp Exchange Ltd [1994] 3 WLR 199

**Key Facts**

Goldcorp Ltd, who were dealers in gold, silver and platinum bullion, were declared bankrupt. Members of the public had sent in orders for bullion but there was insufficient to satisfy all the claims. The customers were in three categories: (1) customers who had not had bullion allocated to them; (2) a single customer who ordered gold coins which had not yet been allocated; (3) customers from an intermediary firm which had been purchased by Goldcorp whose gold bullion had already been segregated into a separate account. The Privy Council held that only the customers in category (3) could trace the assets.

**Key Link**

The gold bullion could only be traced if the goods had been segregated. If the property was to be subject to a trust then it had to be certain and goods which had not been segregated could not be certain. See **Chapter 5.3**.

## 15.4.4 Backwards tracing

### Bishopsgate Investment Management Ltd v Homan [1994] 3 WLR 1270

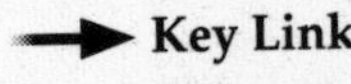

**Key Comment**

It was held in this case that in limited circumstances it may be possible to trace an asset which had been purchased with money from an overdraft or loan. This is sometimes called 'backwards tracing'. It is only possible where it was the intention that the loan was going to be repaid with the misappropriated money.

**Key Link**

This case reaffirms the principle in *Roscoe v Winder* (above).

## 15.4.5 Where trust funds are used to pay off a mortgage

CA

### Boscawen v Bajwa [1996] 1 WLR 328

**Key Facts**

A borrower was lent money by Building Society (A) for the sole purpose of purchasing a house. The money was paid over to the seller prematurely. The sale was not completed but the seller used the money to discharge a mortgage over the property with Building Society (B). The Court of Appeal allowed the claimant Building Society (A) to acquire the mortgage via subrogation. The seller now owed money to Building Society (A) who had stepped into the shoes of Building Society (B).

## 15.4.6 First in, first out

CA

### Clayton's Case, Devaynes v Noble (1816) 1 Mer 529

**Key Facts**

In a current bank account comprising moneys of an innocent volunteer and trust moneys, the first payment in is appropriated to the earliest debt which is not statute-barred. This rule does not apply where the trustee mixes his own money in an account.

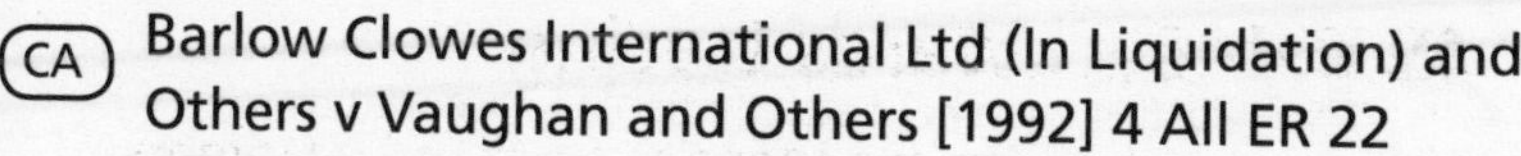

## CA Barlow Clowes International Ltd (In Liquidation) and Others v Vaughan and Others [1992] 4 All ER 22

**Key Facts**

After the Barlow Clowes investment company collapsed the company owed over £115 million. The court decided not to apply Clayton's Case but to share the assets *pari passu*.

**Key Law**

The court held that they were at liberty to depart from the rule when they felt that it would work injustice. In this case the investment fund was regarded by the investors as a common pool and so it was fairer to apply *pari passu* allowing them all to recover some of their money back.

**Key Judgment**

**Woolf LJ:** 'The rule need only be applied when it is convenient to do so … it is not applied if this is the intention or presumed intention of the beneficiaries. The rule is sensibly not applied when the cost of applying it is likely to exhaust the fund available for the beneficiaries.'

# 15.4.7 Tracing against innocent volunteers

## CA Re Diplock [1948] Ch 465

**Key Facts**

A large trust fund was left by Caleb Diplock for various charitable causes. The fund was distributed to the charities but when challenged by the next of kind the beneficiaries under the estate it was found to fail as a charitable trust on strict construction of the wording of the trust document. The next of kin could recover the property through tracing since the charities were in the position of innocent volunteers.

**Key Law**

The charities were held strictly liable to account as constructive trustees for the amounts even though they had acted entirely innocently. However the beneficiaries had first to exhaust all their personal remedies against the executors who had wrongly paid the funds to the charities.

# 16

# Strangers to a Trust

## Who is a stranger to a trust

***Barnes v Addy (1874)***
Strangers are not to be made constructive trustees merely because they act as agents of trustees in transactions within their legal powers unless those agents receive and become chargeable with some part of the trust property or unless they assist with knowledge in a dishonest and fraudulent design on the part of the trustees

## Strangers who take it upon themselves to act as trustees (trustees de son tort)

***Blyth v Fladgate (1891)***
A person who acts as if he were a trustee will be liable as if he had been properly appointed
***Mara v Browne (1896)***

## Strangers who assist in a breach of trust

***Royal Brunei Airlines Sdn v Tan (1995)***
A stranger who had dishonestly assisted in a breach of trust will be liable even where the principal had not acted fraudulently or dishonestly and merely innocently
***Brinks Ltd v Abu-Saleh (No 3) (1995)***
Dishonest assistance cannot be based on passive acquiescence in a breach of trust but can only be brought against someone who knew of the existence of facts giving rise to a trust
***Agip (Africa) Ltd v Jackson (1990)***
**Twinsectra v Yardley (2002)**
The test for dishonesty was a combined test which is both subjective and objective
***Barlow Clowes v Eurotrust International Ltd (2006)***
The test for dishonesty should not allow a defendant to set his own standards for what is dishonest
***Abou-Rahmah v Abachi (2006)***
Suspicions are not enough to prove dishonesty in a stranger to a trust
***Republic of Zambia v Meer Care & Desai (a firm) (2008)***
It is not appropriate to apply a test of competency to dishonesty

## Strangers who receive trust property

***Re Baden Delvaux v Societe General (1983)***
Strangers who receive trust property will only be liable if they come within one of the categories of knowledge ranging from actual knowledge to knowledge of circumstances that would put a guilty man on notice.
***Re Montagu's Settlement Trusts (1987)***
Where a stranger made an honest muddle with property belonging to another he would not be liable as constructive trustee
***Lipkin Gorman (a firm) v Karpnale Ltd (1991)***
A club could not be liable as constructive trustee when they did not have sufficient knowledge of the source of the money received
***Macmillan Inc v Bishopsgate Investment Trust Ltd (1995)***
Those involved in commercial transactions cannot be expected to carry out extensive investigations into the title of property offered for sale.
***BCCI v Akindele (2000)***
The test for knowledge in knowing receipt is unconscionability
***City Index Ltd v Grawler (2008)***

## 16.1 Who is a stranger to the trust?

(CA) Barnes v Addy (1874) 9 Ch App 244

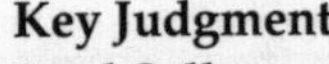

**Key Judgment**

**Lord Selbourne:** 'Strangers are not to be made constructive trustees merely because they act as agents of trustees in transactions within their legal powers, transactions, perhaps of which the Court of Equity may disapprove, unless those agents receive and become chargeable with some part of the trust property, or unless they assist with knowledge in a dishonest and fraudulent design on the part of the trustees…'.

## 16.2 A stranger who takes it upon himself to act as trustee or trustee *de son tort*

(HC) Blyth v Fladgate [1896] 1 Ch 199

**Key Facts**

Solicitors acting for trustees who were all deceased advanced moneys on mortgage from a settlement. The securities proved to be insufficient and the shortfall had to be made good by the solicitors, who had acted as if they were trustees of the funds.

**Key Law**

A person who takes it upon himself to act as an agent for another will be held liable to account to his principal just as if he had been properly appointed.

**Key Judgment**

**Smith LJ:** 'If one, not being a trustee and not having authority from a trustee, takes upon himself to intermeddle with trust matters or to do acts characteristic of the office of trustee, he may thereby make himself what is called in law a trustee of his own wrong, i.e. a trustee *de son tort*, or, as it is also termed, a constructive trustee.'

 Mara v Browne [1896] 1 Ch 199

**Key Facts**

A solicitor advised trustees on some investment decisions. He had not been officially appointed as a trustee. Trust money was lost and the beneficiaries were unable to recover the loss under the rules of negligence because they were time-barred. They argued that the solicitor was a trustee de son tort. The Court of Appeal found the solicitor did not intend or purport to act as a trustee but only as a solicitor to the trustees.

## 16.3 Strangers who assist in a breach of trust

 Royal Brunei Airlines Sdn Bhd v Tan [1995] 2 AC 378

**Key Facts**

The claimants were an airline who used a firm to act as agents in ticket sales. In breach of trust the firm used money from the ticket sales for its own business. The firm became insolvent and Tan, who was the director and principal shareholder, was sued for the proceeds of the sales. The claimants argued that he was an accessory to the breach of trust committed by the now insolvent firm. Tan claimed that he was not liable because although the firm had misused the money, it had neither acted fraudulently nor dishonestly. The court held that he was personally liable for dishonestly assisting in the firm's breach of trust.

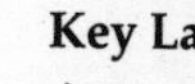

**Key Law**

A stranger can be held to be liable for dishonest assistance in a breach of trust where the breach of trust was neither fraudulent nor dishonest. A stranger can be held liable even where the breach of trust by the trustee is innocent or negligent. The liability of the stranger depends on his personal fault.

**Key Judgment**

**Lord Nicholls:** 'If the liability of the third party is fault-based, what matters is the nature of the fault, not that of the trustee. In this regard dishonesty on the part of the third party would seem to be a sufficient basis for his liability, irrespective of the state of mind of the trustee who is in breach of trust…'.

**Key Comment**

In this case Lord Nicholls emphasised that dishonesty would be judged on an objective standard although there were subjective elements because dishonesty had to be judged in the light of what the defendant knew at the time. However he emphasised that individuals were not free to set their own standards.

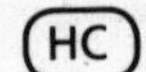

## Brinks Ltd v Abu-Saleh (No 3) [1995] 1 WLR 1478

**Key Facts**

A large quantity of gold bullion was stolen from a warehouse at Heathrow. Civil proceedings were brought against certain persons whom it was alleged had been involved in the robbery and the subsequent laundering operations. Proceedings were brought against Mrs E whom it was alleged had knowingly assisted her husband in a breach of trust. She had accompanied him on subsequent trips to Switzerland to launder part of the proceeds of the robbery. The court held that Mrs E had not assisted in a breach of trust because she was not aware of the real purpose of the trips. She thought that the money was the subject of a tax evasion scheme.

**Key Law**

Dishonest assistance cannot be based on passive acquiescence in a breach of trust. The claim can only be brought against someone who knew of the existence of the trust or facts giving rise to a trust.

## (HL) Twinsectra v Yardley [2002] 2 All ER 377

**Key Facts**

Twinsectra agreed to lend money on certain terms to Mr Yardley, a businessman. They advanced the money to Sims, solicitors acting on behalf of Mr Yardley, on an undertaking that the fund would be applied solely in the acquisition of specified property. Mr Leach an independent solicitor also acting for Mr Yardley received the money from Sims. Contrary to the undertaking the money was advanced to Yardley without ensuring it was used to purchase property. It was used for other purposes by Yardley and never repaid. Twinsectra claimed the money had been held on trust for them by the first set of solicitors and Mr Leach had dishonestly assisted them in a breach of trust and was personally liable for the loss. The House of Lords held that he was not liable for dishonestly assisting in the breach of trust.

**Key Law**

The judge at first instance (Carnwath J) held that the money had not been held on trust and L had not acted dishonestly.

The Court of Appeal held there was a trust and L had acted dishonestly.

The House of Lords held that there was a trust, but by a majority they held that L had not acted dishonestly.

**Key Judgment**

**Lord Hutton:** 'There is a purely subjective standard, whereby a person is only regarded as dishonest if he transgresses his own standard of honesty; even if that standard is contrary to that of reasonable and honest people … there is a purely objective standard whereby a person acts dishonestly if his conduct is dishonest by the ordinary standards of reasonable and honest people, even if he does not realise this; thirdly there is a standard which combines an objective and a subjective test, and which requires that before there can be a finding of dishonesty it must be established that the defendant's conduct was dishonest by the standards of reasonable and honest people and that he himself realised that by those standards his conduct was dishonest. I will call this "the combined test".'

*Twinsectra v Yardley* held that the standard of dishonesty necessary for the imposition of accessory liability is the combined test.

## PC Barlow Clowes International Ltd (in liquidation) v Eurotrust International Ltd and others [2006] 1 AER 33

**Key Facts**

The defendant was a Director of Eurotrust, a company operating in the Isle of Man providing offshore services. Money misappropriated from investors was placed with the company. The Director of Eurotrust strongly suspected that the money had been stolen but had not made inquiries. He argued that he was not dishonest on the basis of the test from Twinsectra because he had not been aware that his actions were dishonest by ordinary standards.

The court held that the defendant was liable. It was not necessary for the claimants to prove that he had actually considered what normally acceptable standards of honest conduct might be.

## CA Abou-Rahmah v Abacha [2006] EWCA Civ 1492

**Key Facts**

This case concerned money-laundering. The claimant was a lawyer practising in Kuwait. He had been a victim of a fraud. He sought to recover some money which he had transferred to a bank on instruction from the fraudsters. He argued that the bank had dishonestly assisted in the breach of trust and was liable. The local bank manager admitted that he was suspicious that the fraudsters were involved in money laundering but there was nothing in the transaction itself to make him unduly suspicious. The Court of Appeal held that the bank was not liable.

## AG of Zambia v Meer Care & Desai [2008] EWCA Civ 1007

**Key Facts**

The Court of Appeal reviewed the test for dishonesty. A solicitor responsible for handling large sums of money in a client account belonging to the former president of Zambia was held to have had acted with poor judgment but not dishonestly. He could only be held liable if he had clear suspicions about a transaction and then ignored these suspicions even if he had not considered whether in so doing he was transgressing ordinary standards

**Key Judgment**

**Lloyd LJ:** '… the judge relied heavily on the test of what an honest solicitor would have done or … whether an honest solicitor could have done that which Mr Meer did, given the bench mark of the honest and competent solicitor … that hypothetical comparator is not appropriate, because it assumes that Mr Meer was competent … It seems to us that the judge failed to give adequate consideration to the possibility that Mr Meer was honest but not competent and was not in truth knowledgeable or experienced in relation to the sort of transaction with which he was faced … .'

# 16.4 Strangers who receive trust property in breach of trust

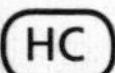

## Re Baden Delvaux v Société General [1983] BCLC 325

**Key Facts**

The defendant bank was not held liable as constructive trustees for the transfer of moneys to an account which was not designated as a trust account, which had then been dissipated.

**Key Law**

There are five classes of knowledge:

(i) actual knowledge;
(ii) wilfully shutting one's eyes to the obvious;
(iii) wilfully and recklessly failing to make such inquiries as an honest and reasonable man would make;

(iv) knowledge of circumstances which would indicate the facts to an honest and reasonable man;
(v) knowledge of circumstances which would put an honest and reasonable man on inquiry.

**Key Comment**

Recent cases (see *Re Montagu* below) suggest that classes (i)–(iii) will generally give rise to liability, but classes (iv)–(v) derive from negligence and will not generally give rise to liability as a constructive trustee.

## BCCI Ltd v Akindele [2000] 4 All ER 221

**Key Facts**

The defendant received money as a return on an invalid loan. The liquidators claimed this sum on the basis that he had dishonestly received it and therefore held it as a constructive trustee. He did not know that the loan was fraudulent nor the other frauds that were being perpetrated within the group.

**Key Law**

He was not held liable to account as constructive trustee of the monies, since he had not acted unconscionably.

**Key Judgment**

**Nourse LJ:** 'I have come to the view that, just as there is now a single test of dishonesty for knowing assistance, so ought there to be a single test of knowledge for knowing receipt. The recipient's state of knowledge must be such as to make it unconscionable for him to retain the benefit of the receipt…'.

## City Index Ltd v Gawler [2008] Ch 313

**Key Judgment**

'It is accepted that Akindele represents the present law. Accordingly liability for "knowing receipt" depends on the defendant having sufficient knowledge of the circumstances of the payment to make it "unconscionable" for him to retain the benefit or pay it away for his own purposes.'

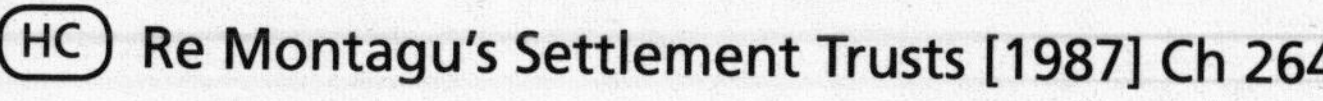

## (HC) Re Montagu's Settlement Trusts [1987] Ch 264

**Key Facts**

The 10th Duke of Manchester received a large number of chattels from a family trust. He sold a number of them believing them to be his own. On his death it was found that he had sold items that should have passed to the 11th Duke of Manchester, who claimed that the 10th Duke had held them as constructive trustee and should have to personally account for them to him.

**Key Law**

It was held that he was not personally liable as a constructive trustee for the items because he did not have subjective knowledge of the breach.

## (HL) Lipkin Gorman (a firm) v Karpnale Ltd [1991] 3 WLR 10

**Key Facts**

A solicitor used money from his firm's client account to gamble at the Playboy Club. The firm later tried to recover this money, alleging the club were constructive trustees of the money received. The money had ceased to be identifiable under the rules of tracing.

**Key Law**

The court held that the club had not received the money with sufficient knowledge in order to make it accountable as a constructive trustee.

# 17

# *Variation of a Trust*

**The rule in *Saunders v Vautier***

If all the beneficiaries are *sui juris* and in agreement and together have absolute entitlement they have power to terminate the trust and demand the fund be handed over to them

***Re Smith (1928)***

**Variation under the court's inherent jurisdiction**

***Chapman v Chapman (1954)***

The court has power to vary the terms of a trust

**Variation of a Trust**

**Variation under the Variations of Trusts Act 1958**

***Re Suffert (1961)***

Consent cannot be sought on behalf of persons who are not within s 1 of the Variation of Trusts Act. If they do not give their consent or cannot be found the trust cannot be varied

***Knocker v Youle (1986)***

The court cannot give consent on behalf of beneficiaries who were outside s 1(1)(b) who had existing beneficial interests

**The meaning of benefit**

***Re Weston's Settlement (1969)***

Benefit was not restricted to financial benefit. Social benefits could be seen as more important

***Re Holt's Settlement (1969) Re Remnant's Settlement Trusts (1970)***

**The settlor's wishes and the purpose of the trust**

***Goulding v James (1997)***

The settlor's wishes are not relevant to the decision of the court in a variation of trust application

***Re Steed's Will Trusts (1960)***

***Re T's Settlement Trust (1964)***

***Wyndham v Egremont (2009)***

***Ridgwell v Ridgwell (2007)***

## 17.1 The rule in *Saunders v Vautier*

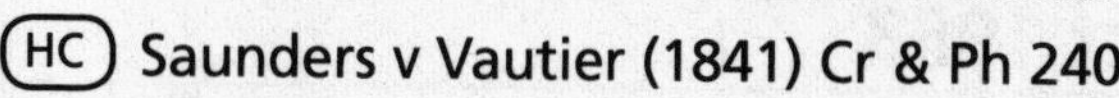

### (HC) Saunders v Vautier (1841) Cr & Ph 240

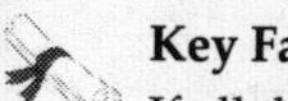

**Key Facts**

If all the beneficiaries are sui juris and in agreement and together have absolute entitlement, they have power to terminate the trust and demand that the fund be handed over to them.

### (HC) Re Smith [1928] Ch 915

**Key Law**

The beneficiaries of a discretionary trust can compel the trustees to transfer the legal title to them.

## 17.2 Variation under the court's inherent jurisdiction

### (CA) Chapman v Chapman [1954] AC 429

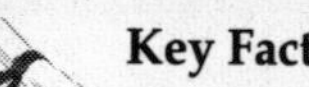

**Key Facts**

There are four situations where the court has the power to vary the terms of a trust:

1. conversion of personalty to realty;
2. emergency jurisdiction, where the court can authorise transactions not included in the trust instrument but cannot vary the interests of the beneficiaries;
3. maintenance jurisdiction allowing the court power to advance income to the beneficiaries for their maintenance;
4. compromise jurisdiction allowing variation in the beneficial interests of the beneficiaries where there is a dispute about the extent of the rights of the beneficiaries.

# 17.3 Variation under the Variation of Trusts Act 1958

## HC Re Suffert [1961] Ch 1

**Key Facts**

A trust was established giving a lifetime interest for Elaine Suffert and remainder to such of those issue as she should appoint. If she died intestate then the property would pass to those entitled on her intestacy. She was a spinster and had no children but three adult cousins. She wanted to vary the settlement, but only one cousin consented. The court held that they had no jurisdiction to vary on their behalf as they were not persons who 'would become entitled at a future date'.

**Key Law**

Consent from the court cannot be sought on behalf of persons who are not within s 1 Variation of Trusts Act; if they do not give their consent or cannot be found then the trust cannot be varied.

## HC Knocker v Youle [1986] 1 WLR 934

**Key Facts**

A variation was sought in a trust where beneficiaries had remote contingent interests and as they were abroad and numerous, for practical reasons, they would not be able to give their approval. The court held that under the Variation of Trusts Act the court was unable to give their consent on their behalf because they had existing contingent interests and s 1(1)(b) only covered those who may become entitled to an interest.

### 17.3.1 Interpretation of benefits

## CA Re Weston's Settlement [1969] 1 Ch 223

**Key Facts**

A variation was sought for infant beneficiaries of a settlement which would transfer the whole of the trust to Jersey. There was a considerable financial benefit to be gained by doing so, but the court thought that the social benefits for the children in remaining in England far outweighed these financial benefits.

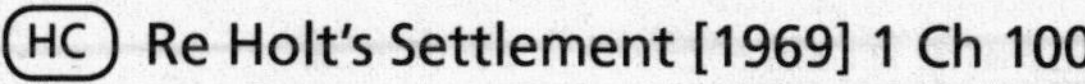

## (HC) Re Holt's Settlement [1969] 1 Ch 100

**Key Facts**

A variation was approved where the interests of the beneficiaries were postponed until they attained the age of 30. It was felt that it was important that they should not receive the income until they were reasonably advanced in their careers and settled in life.

**Key Law**

Benefit under the Variation of Trusts Act 1958 should be given a wide definition. It is not merely confined to financial benefit, but may extend to 'moral or social benefit'.

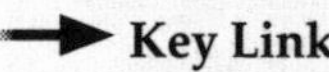

**Key Link**

Consider the formalities necessary under the Variation of Trusts Act. Megarry J held in *Re Holt's Settlement* that s 53(1)(c) did not apply on a variation leading to a disposition of an existing beneficial interest.

## (HC) Ridgwell v Ridgwell [2007] EWHC 2666

**Key Facts**

The court balanced the long-term tax benefits of a variation with the effects of postponing the entitlement of current and unborn children and held the tax advantages outweighed the disadvantages.

# 17.3.2 Variation or resettlement?

## (HC) Re T's Settlement Trusts [1964] Ch 158

**Key Facts**

Mr Justice Wilberforce refused an application for a variation of a trust preventing an infant from receiving a quarter of the income on attaining her majority although there was evidence that the child was irresponsible and immature because he believed the variation amounted to a complete resettlement of the trust.

**Key Comment**

The court took a different view in *Re Holt* (see **above**), where the children's entitlements were postponed until they attained the age of 30.

**Key Link**

See **Chapter 4**.

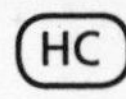

## Re Balls' Settlement Trusts [1968] 1 WLR 899

**Key Facts**

A test was laid down intended to guide the judiciary in applications under the VTA. It was held that an arrangement changing the whole substratum of the trust would not be regarded as a variation but if the substratum was unaffected the court could give consent.

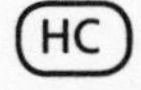

## Wyndham v Egremont [2009] EWHC 2076 (Ch)

**Key Facts**

A variation of a family trust was drawn up to defer tax liability. It was intended to maintain the original purpose of the trust which was to ensure that the Petworth estate continued to pass to male heirs of a family. The court concluded that this was not a resettlement and could therefore be approved. The statement in *Re Ball's Settlement* was criticised because it did not give sufficient guidance on the difference between a variation and a resettlement.

# 17.3.3 Relevance of the settlor's intention to the variation?

## Goulding v James [1997] 2 All ER 239

**Key Facts**

An estate was left by the testatrix for her daughter for life, with the remainder to her grandson on his attaining the age of 40. If he failed to attain the age of 40 then it was provided that the estate should pass to such of his children as were living at the date of his death. The testatrix did not trust her son-in-law and thought her grandson needed to settle down before he inherited the capital. The trust was varied allowing the daughter to receive some capital and the grandson to become entitled before the age of 40. This was clearly contrary to the wishes of the settlor.

**Key Law**

The settlor's intentions in the variation of a trust on behalf of unborn beneficiaries are not relevant to the decision of the court.

**Key Judgment**

**Ralph Gibson LJ:** 'The fact that a testator would not have approved or would have disapproved very strongly does not alter the fact that the beneficiaries are entitled in law to do it and, if it can be proved, that the arrangement is for the benefit of the unborn ...'.

## Re Steed's Will Trusts [1960] Ch 407

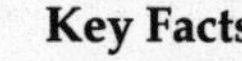

**Key Facts**

A farm had been left on trust for the testator's faithful housekeeper for her life on protective trusts and on her death to whoever she should appoint. The trustees had the power to pay capital monies to her as they should think fit. The testator had left a protective trust believing that her family may take advantage of her. She exercised her power of appointment to herself but under the protective trust she could not resist decisions of the trustees. She sought an order to vary the arrangement after the trustees decided to sell a farm rented by one of her brothers. The variation would give her absolute entitlement to the property. The court refused to vary the trust taking into account the wishes of the settlor.

**Key Judgment**

**Lord Evershed:** 'The court must, in performing its duty under the Variation of Trusts Act 1958, regard the proposal in the light of the purpose of the trust as shown by the evidence of the will or settlement itself and any other relevant evidence available…'.

**Key Problem**

Compare the decisions in Re Steed and Goulding v James. The court were guided by the settlor's wishes in Re Steed. Perhaps the reason for this was as the Court of Appeal said: it is the arrangement that has to be approved, not just the interest of the person on whose behalf the court's duty is to consider it.

## (HC) Re Remnant's Settlement Trusts [1970] Ch 560

**Key Facts**

A variation was sought to a settlement which contained a forfeiture clause forfeiting interests of members of the family who became or who married Roman Catholics. The variation removing this clause was approved by the court. There was a benefit to the children and retention of the clause was undesirable.

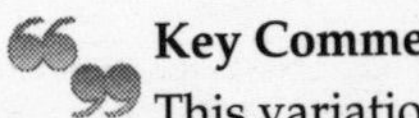

**Key Comment**

This variation defeated the settlor's intention, but although that was a serious matter, the benefit to the trust outweighed this.

# 18

# *Remedies*

## Specific performance

No order for specific performance can be made which requires constant supervision from the court

***Ryan v Mutual Tontine Westminster Chambers Association (1893)***

***Co-operative Insurance v Argyll (1997)***

***Posner v Scott-Lewis (1987)***

If constant supervision is not necessary then a decree of specific performance will be granted

***Verrall v Great Yarmouth Borough Council (1981)***

Specific performance can be granted to enforce any interest in land including a contractual licence

***Price v Strange (1978)***

Specific performance is normally only granted where both parties can perform their part of the bargain but occasionally it will be granted where there is no mutuality

## Injunctions

**Protection of the claimant's rights**

***Paton v British Pregnancy Advisory Service Trustees (1979)***

An injunction will only be granted where the claimant could show that his lawful rights had been infringed

**Injunctions are discretionary**

***Wrotham Park Estate Co Ltd v Parkside Homes Ltd (1974)***

An injunction may not automatically be granted since it is a discretionary remedy

***Fisher v Brooker (1979)***

## Defences

**Mistake**

***Patel v Ali (1984)***

Specific performance will not be granted where it would cause hardship

**Delay**

***Lazard Brothers & Co Ltd v Fairfield Property Co (Mayfair) Ltd (1977)***

Specific performance can be granted even where there has been some delay so long as it is not excessive

## Interlocutory injunctions

***American Cyanamid Co v Ethicon (1975)***

An interlocutory injunction will be granted where there is a serious issue to be tried and the court has weighed the balance of convenience and taken other factors into account

## Mareva injunctions/ freezing orders

***Mareva Compania Naviera v International Bulk Carriers SA (1975)***

This case lays down the circumstances allowing the grant of a freezing order

***Derby & Co v Weldon (1990)***

Freezing orders can be made worldwide and are not limited to assets in the United Kingdom

***Anton Piller Orders/ Search Orders***

***Anton Piller KG v Manufacturing Processes Ltd (1976)***

This case lays down the conditions for the grant by the court of a search order

## 18.1 Specific performance

### (HL) Co-operative Insurance v Argyll [1997] 3 All ER 297

**Key Facts**

The defendants had covenanted within their lease to keep the premises open for 'retail trade'. They leased a shop in a shopping centre. They decided that the shop should be closed as part of a national reorganisation and the claimants sought to rely on the covenant. The decree was not granted; although the breach was deliberate, the grant of a decree of specific performance would be oppressive to the tenant whose loss in complying with the order would be far greater than the loss to the landlord should the covenant be broken.

**Key Law**

The defendants could not be expected to conduct an activity which would require constant supervision by the court.

**Key Judgment**

**Lord Hoffman:** 'It was orthodox doctrine that the power to decree specific performance was part of the discretionary jurisdiction of the Court of Chancery to do justice in cases in which the remedies available at common law were inadequate.'

### (CA) Ryan v Mutual Tontine Westminster Chambers Association [1893] 1 Ch 116

**Key Facts**

The defendants had agreed to provide a porter for a block of residential flats which they owned. A decree of specific performance was refused, because it would involve constant supervision by the court.

### (HC) Posner v Scott-Lewis [1987] Ch 25

**Key Facts**

The defendants had covenanted to provide a residential porter purely for maintenance and cleaning of the property. This was enforceable by a decree of specific performance because it did not require constant supervision in order to be enforced and it was felt that the remedy of damages was inadequate.

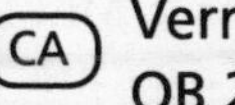


## Verrall v Great Yarmouth Borough Council [1981] QB 202

**Key Facts**

The defendant council had repudiated a contract allowing the National Front a contractual licence to occupy premises owned by them for two days for its National Conference. The court granted a decree of specific performance although the National Front only had a contractual licence to enjoy the land. This was because specific performance can always be granted in any contract involving land.

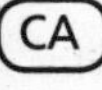


## Price v Strange [1978] Ch 337

**Key Facts**

The defendant had agreed to grant the claimant a new lease if he would carry out certain repairs both internally and externally. The internal repairs had been carried out, but not the external repairs, because the defendant had already completed them herself. Specific performance could not have been granted to the defendant. The order was granted to the claimant in spite of the lack of mutuality.

# 18.1.1 Defences

### Mistake

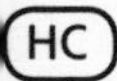


## Webster v Cecil (1861) 30 Beav 62

**Key Facts**

A offered to sell B some property for £1,250. This was a mistake as he had intended to sell at £2,250. B agreed to buy at £1,250 but the court refused to grant an order for specific performance and A was not compelled to sell at that price because there had been a genuine mistake, known to the claimant.

### Hardship

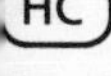


## Patel v Ali [1984] Ch 283

**Key Facts**

Mr and Mrs Ali had exchanged contracts with Mr and Mrs Patel, agreeing to sell them their house. A series of events, including the bankruptcy of Mr Ali and his subsequent imprisonment, Mrs Ali then contracting cancer leading to the amputation of a leg just before the birth of their second child and followed by the birth of a third child, meant they could not complete. The court did not grant an order for specific performance because of the hardship that it would cause them.

### Delay

CA

### Lazard Brothers & Co Ltd v Fairfield Property Co (Mayfair) Ltd (1977) 121 SJ 793

**Key Facts**

The claimants sought to enforce a contract for sale two years after it had been drawn up. The court held that they could not refuse to grant the remedy merely because the claimants had been guilty of some delay. The order should be made if it was just that the claimants should be granted the remedy.

# 18.2 Injunctions

## 18.2.1 Protection of the claimant's rights

HC

### Paton v British Pregnancy Advisory Service Trustees [1979] QB 276

**Key Facts**

A husband sought an injunction to prevent his pregnant wife from having an abortion. This was refused because he had no lawful right that had been infringed.

## 18.2.2 Discretionary nature of injunctions

HC

### Wrotham Park Estate Co Ltd v Parkside Homes Ltd [1974] 1 WLR 798

**Key Facts**

A number of houses had been built in contravention of a restrictive covenant. An application was made for a mandatory injunction.

This was not granted by the court because they felt it would be 'a waste of much needed houses'. Instead, damages were granted which were substantially more than that which would have been granted at common law, because the actual loss to the claimant was purely nominal, as the value of his own house had not been reduced.

## 18.2.3 Delay and acquiescence

### HL Fisher v Brooker [2009] 1 WLR 1764

**Key Facts**

A very successful record was released in 1965 by Procul Harum. In 2005 one of the composers who had never received royalties because his contribution had never been acknowledged sought to enforce his rights. The House of Lords held that he was not debarred from bringing an action in spite of the long delay. However the delay would be relevant to the issue of the grant of an injunction against future exploitation of his work.

## 18.2.4 Interlocutory injunctions

### HL American Cyanamid Co v Ethicon Ltd [1975] AC 295

**Key Facts**

The case concerned an application for an injunction to restrain the infringement of a patent. It was held that there was no rule which required the claimant to prove a *prima facie* case.

A number of factors must be taken into account before a court will grant an interlocutory injunction:

(i) Is there a serious issue to be tried? The claim must not be frivolous or vexatious.

(ii) The balance of convenience. The court must weigh the balance of convenience between granting and refusing an injunction.

(iii) Other factors to be taken into account.

## 18.2.5 Freezing injunctions

### Mareva Compania Naviera SA v International Bulk Carriers SA [1975] 2 Lloyd's Rep 509

**Key Comment**

It was first introduced as a Mareva injunction after the decision in the above case; now it has been renamed a freezing order under the Civil Procedure Rules. The order freezes assets preventing the defendant from dissipating or removing them from the jurisdiction.

### Derby & Co v Weldon [1990] Ch 48

**Key Law**

The courts are prepared to grant a world-wide order under very strict conditions. The claimant must show that any English assets are insufficient and that there are foreign assets and there is real risk of dissipation if the foreign assets are not frozen.

## 18.2.6 Search orders

### Anton Piller KG v Manufacturing Processes Ltd [1976] Ch 55

This is an order requiring the defendant to permit the claimant to enter the defendant's premises for specified purposes. This is usually for the preservation of evidence.

**Key Law**

There are three conditions for granting such an order:

(i) strong *prima facie* case;
(ii) serious potential damage;
(iii) real possibility evidence will be destroyed.

A further condition was added later that an order would do no real harm to the defendant.

# Index

*Indexer: Dr Laurence Errington*